Breaking the Jaws of Silence

Breaking the Jaws of Silence

✦ ✦ ✦

SIXTY AMERICAN POETS
SPEAK TO THE WORLD

Edited by Sholeh Wolpé

The University of Arkansas Press
Fayetteville
2013

ISBN-10: 1-55728-629-9
ISBN-13: 978-1-55728-629-1

17 16 15 14 13   5 4 3 2 1

Text design by Ellen Beeler

♾The paper used in this publication meets the minimum requirements of the American National Standard for Permanence of Paper for Printed Library Materials Z39.48-1984.

Library of Congress Cataloging-in-Publication Data

Breaking the jaws of silence : sixty American poets speak to the world / edited by Sholeh Wolpé.
    pages cm
    Includes bibliographical references.
    ISBN 978-1-55728-629-1 — ISBN 1-55728-629-9
    1. Protest poetry, American. 2. Human rights—Poetry. 3. Liberty—Poetry.
    4. Freedom of expression—Poetry. 5. American poetry—21st century.
    6. American poetry—20th century. I. Wolpé, Sholeh, editor of compilation.
    PS593.P77B74 2013
    811'.60803581—dc23
                                                                2012045632

Dedicated to you, because the
world is one country
and poetry its language.

"We humanize what is going on in the world and in ourselves only by speaking of it, and in the course of speaking of it we learn to be human."

—*Hannah Arendt,* Men in Dark Times

Contents

Editor's Note

Consider this: "We don't want war. We just want freedom." This said by a twenty-seven-year-old protestor as she marched in a peaceful protest in the streets of Tehran. Isn't this what most people in this world want? Yet freedom has to be fought for.

Carolyn Forché in her groundbreaking anthology *Against Forgetting* writes, "One of the things that I believe happens when poets bear witness to historical events is that everyone they tell also becomes responsible for what they have heard and what they now know." It was in this spirit that through PEN USA I called on sixty prominent American poets to raise their voices in unison against the whirlwind of oppression that has polluted our world. It is time to fight the way we as poets know how: to bear witness, to collectively engage, to activate, to call, to give texture, to demand, to caress, to shatter, to build, and to never let the world forget.

In the words of the great Arab poet Mahmoud Darwish, "Against barbarity, poetry can resist only by confirming its attachment to human fragility like a blade of grass growing on a wall while armies march by."

From Damascus to Beijing to Tehran in every revolution or uprising, poets are among the first to be jailed. But the voice of the poet cannot be arrested. Like rain their words seep into every crevice where people have been driven underground and feed the seedlings that eventually break through the cracks in the streets, squares and walls of their countries, changing the landscape despite oppression, torture, and denial of the most basic human rights.

In this collection, sixty prominent American poets speak in unison addressing the world through poems that not only meditate on the principles of freedom, justice, and tolerance but also boldly and directly address specific countries. All the poems have been gifted to this anthology so that a portion of the proceeds benefits PEN Center USA, an organization dedicated to creating a world in which freedom of expression is guaranteed for all writers.

Poets are a threat to despotic regimes as light is a threat to darkness. Yet consider this: light is most brilliant when it travels through darkness. Here you will find some of this light.

Foreword

See Them Coming

Here come the octopi of war
tentacles wielding guns, missiles
holy books and colorful flags.

Don't fill your pens with their ink.
Write with your fingernails, scratch
light upon these darkened days.

Sholeh Wolpé

Breaking the Jaws of Silence

ROBERT BLY

Call and Answer

August 2002

Tell me why it is we don't lift our voices these days
and cry over what is happening. Have you noticed
the plans are made for Iraq and the ice cap is melting?

I say to myself: "Go on, cry. What's the sense
of being an adult and having no voice? Cry out!
see who will answer! *This is Call and Answer!*"

We will have to call especially loud to reach
our angels, who are hard of hearing; they are hiding
in the jugs of silence filled during our wars.

Have we agreed to so many wars that we can't
escape from silence? If we don't lift our voices, we allow
others (who are ourselves) to rob the house.

How come we've listened to the great criers—Neruda,
Akhmatova, Thoreau, Frederick Douglass—and now
we're silent as sparrows in the little bushes?

Some masters say our life lasts only seven days.
Where are we in the week? Is it Thursday yet?
Hurry, cry now! Soon Sunday night will come.

RITA DOVE

Lady Freedom among Us

don't lower your eyes
or stare straight ahead to where
you think you ought to be going

don't mutter *oh no*
not another one
get a job   fly a kite
go bury a bone

with her oldfashioned sandals
with her leaden skirts
with her stained cheeks and whiskers and heaped up trinkets
she has risen among us in blunt reproach

she has fitted her hair under a hand-me-down cap
and spruced it up with feathers and stars
slung over one shoulder she bears
the rainbowed layers of charity and murmurs
all of you   even the least of you

don't cross to the other side of the square
don't think *another item to fit on a tourist's agenda*

consider her drenched gaze   her shining brow
she who has brought mercy back into the streets
and will not retire politely to the potter's field

having assumed the thick skin of this town
its gritted exhaust its sunscorch and blear

she rests in her weathered plumage
bigboned   resolute

don't think you can ever forget her
don't even try
she's not going to budge

no choice but to grant her space
crown her with sky
for she is one of the many
and she is each of us

Your Beauty Is Overwhelming

Taking to the streets
Taking a risk
Marching with placards
Objecting
Wearing white shirts
On the other side of the world
You can't hear us cheering for you
We can't hear the conversations in your kitchens
What else are people supposed to do with voices?
But use them? Use them? Use them?

YUSEF KOMUNYAKAA

Green

I've known billy club, tear gas, & cattle prod,
but not Black Sheep killing White Sheep.
I've known high-pressure water hoses
& the subterranean cry of a Black Maria
rounding a city corner on two angry wheels,
but couldn't smell cedar taking root in the air.

I've known of secret graves guarded
by the night owl in oak & poplar.
I've known police dogs on choke chains.
I've known how "We Shall Overcome"
feels on a half-broken tongue,
but not how deeply sunsets wounded the Peacock throne.

Because of what I never dreamt
I know Hafez's litany balanced on Tamerlane's saber,
a gholam's song limping up the Alborz Mountains—
no, let's come back first to *now*,
to a surge of voices shouting,
"Death to the government of potato!"

Back to the iron horses of the Basijis
galloping through days whipped bloody
& beaten back into the brain's cave
louder than a swarm of percussion
clobbered in Enghelab Square,
cries bullied into alleyways & cutoff.

Though each struck bell goes on
mumbling in the executioner's sleep,
there are always two hands holding
on to earth, & I believe their faith
in tomorrow's million green flags waving
could hold back a mile of tanks & turn

the Revolutionary Guard into stone,
that wherever a clue dares to step
a seed is pressed into damp soil.
A shoot, a tendril, the tip of a wing.
One breath at a time, it holds till it is
uprooted, or torn from its own grip.

ELOISE KLEIN HEALY

On Reading a Biography of George Washington

There is no cherry tree.
There is mud and blood and winter.

There are letters and orders to his farm manager
written by candle light detailing chores to do.

There are letters written to his British broker
complaining about low prices for his corn.

There is nothing lofty written about democracy
but there is something about the country

he surveyed beyond the mountains.
There is nothing about democracy yet

but he is tired of being told what
he can and cannot do.

Tired. Of a King.

Of being told what he can
and cannot do in his country.

There is a letter in which he orders
a uniform he designed himself.

It does not fit very well
because he does not know his size.

He wears it anyway.
Democracy.

Design and redesign and self-design.
Democracy.

Something lofty was written
in mud and blood and winters.
Democracy.

WILLIS BARNSTONE

End of the War, 1949

In a dark pool hall, the ghosts sip sweet coffee,
an amputee smokes, whistles as he eyeballs

and shoots for the pocket. He wins an ouzo
and hops outside to the King's Park at Zappeion

where sun falls in the still rooms of a bird's ear,
but no one bothers the marble ghost on the hill.

The Parthenon is sleepy and abandoned.
I meander a bit on cloudy sand

out to olive groves who wrestle an ax.
Herons rise in terror from the big guns,

cemeteries can't care about the dead
or feel the dark drum in the cypresses,

and the dead walk about but fail to show.
The amputees stroll, twirling worry beads

and wear a carnation in their kouros lips
all morning in memory of hostages in trucks.

Athens, 1949

GARRETT HONGO

Kubota to Miguel Hernandez in Heaven, Leupp, Arizona, 1942

The sun travels slowly from over the top of this adobe stockade
And, when I finally wake and pull my face to the bars
At my window, I see a gray light filling in the shadows
Between the mess and guard quarters
And among river stones on the sides of the central well.
Horses snort and whinny far off from the corral I cannot see,
And a line of burros shuffles by, led by a single Navajo
Dressed in khaki-colored clothes from the trading post.
I've been here two months now, can name the hills
Surrounding this plateau of piñon pines—words I learned
From the guards and other prisoners, Japanese like me
Swept up in the days after the attack on Pearl Harbor.
The guards won't say what our crime is, rarely address us,
But I overhear them sometimes, saying the names of mountains,
Nearby towns, complaining about food and us "Japs."
They won't say if we'll be let go. The interrogators come
Every few days and ask about our hobbies back home—
Studying poetry, working the short wave radio at night,
And me, how I go night fishing for *kumu* on Kahuku Point.
What landed me here was I used to go torching,
Wrapping the kerosene-soaked rags on bamboo poles,
Sticking them into the sand inside the lagoon,
And then go light them with a flick from my Zippo.
The fish come in from outside the reef,
Schooling to the light, and me I catch enough
To feed my neighbors—Portagee, Hawaiian, Chinee, and all—
Eating good for days after, like New Year's in early December.
For this they say I'm signaling submarines offshore,

Telling the Japanese navy the south-southwest route to Pearl.
That's a lie. They ask when—I tell them. They ask where—I tell them.
How many fish?—I tell them same every time. No change my answer.
But how can you transform your sorrow into poems, Miguel?
To think of your wife and infant son with only onions to eat,
While you sing your lullabies from your cell in Alicante?
Is it cold for you, Miguel? With only the dark to wrap yourself in?
It is warm, even hot here on Navajo land in northern Arizona,
Where your poems descend to me in the moon's sweet, silver light
As it rises over the Mogollon Plateau these summer evenings.
They say that your sentence was death for writing poetry,
That you celebrated the Republic and the commoners.
I celebrated only my family and the richness of the sea.
My sentence, therefore, is only eternity to wait, not knowing,
Imagining *everything,* imagining nothing—
My wife taking in boarders, doing their laundry and sewing,
My children growing more trivial by the day
Without word where I have been taken,
Whether I will be returned or simply have vanished
Into the unwritten history of our country.
Your suffering tells me to be patient, Miguel,
To think of your song of sweet onions lulling your baby,
Even in his hunger, to a peaceful sleep,
While the wars of our time, and their ignorant ministrations,
Go on shedding their black, tyrannical light into the future.

BRIAN TURNER

Night in Blue

At seven thousand feet and looking back, running lights
blacked out under the wings and America waiting,
a year of my life disappears at midnight,
the sky a deep viridian, the houselights below
small as match heads burned down to embers.

Has this year made me a better lover?
Will I understand something of hardship,
of loss, will a lover sense this
in my kiss or touch? What do I know
of redemption or sacrifice, what will I have
to say of the dead—that it was worth it,
that any of it made sense?
I have no words to speak of war.
I never dug the graves in Talafar.
I never held the mother crying in Ramadi.
I never lifted my friend's body
when they carried him home.

I have only the shadows under the leaves
to take with me, the quiet of the desert,
the low fog of Balad, orange groves
with ice forming on the rinds of fruit.
I have a woman crying in my ear
late at night when the stars go dim,
moonlight and sand as a resonance
of the dust of bones, and nothing more.

ANNIE FINCH

This Place is Here

A dialogue with the YouTube video "Poem from the rooftops of Iran,"
posted June 19, 2009

Friday the 19th of June 2009
Tomorrow, Saturday

Tomorrow is a day of destiny
Tonight, the cries of Allah-o Akbar
are heard louder and louder than the nights before

(and our cries are louder too)

Where is this place?

(It is with us)

Where is this place where every door is closed?

(It is with us)

Where is this place where people are simply calling God?
Where is this place where the sound
of Allah-o Akbar gets louder and louder?

Where is this place?

I wait every night to see if the sounds
will get louder and whether the number increases

(We wait every night
for your voices,
your words,
your poems)

It shakes me

(We see the lights in the darkness from your roof
We shake with you
we cry to hear your voice)

I wonder if God is shaken

(we shake with you)

Where is this place where
so many innocent people are entrapped?
Where is this place where no one comes to our aid?

(It is our world too)

Where is this place where only with our silence
we are sending our voices to the world?

(Your silence shakes us.
Your voice shakes us)

Where is this place where the young shed blood
and then people go and pray?
Standing on that same blood and pray . . .
Where is this place where the citizens
  are called vagrants?
Where is this place? You want me to tell you?
This place is Iran.
The homeland of you and me

(The homeland of you and me.)

This place is Iran.

(The homeland of you and me.)
(Tomorrow is a day of destiny.)

Tienanmen, The Aftermath

There was blood and guts all over the road.
I said I'm sorry, darling, and rolled over,
expecting the slate to be clean; but she came,
she who was never alive became resurrected.
I saw her in dream . . . a young girl in a *qipao*,
bespeckled, forever lingering, thriving
on the other side of the world, walking in my soles
as I walked, crying in my voice as I cried. When
she arrived, I felt my knuckles in her knock,
her light looming over the city's great hollows.

Hope lies within another country's semaphores.
The Goddess of Liberty, the Statue of Mercy—
we have it all wrong—big boy, how we choose to love,
how we choose to destroy, says Zhuangzi, is written
in heaven—but leave the innocent ones alone,
those alive, yet stillborn, undead, yet waiting
in a fitful sleep undeserved of an awakening.

JOY HARJO

In Mystic

For Pam Uschuk

My path is the burning trees,
Lit up by crows with fire in their mouths.
I ask the guardians of these lands for permission to enter.
I am a visitor to this history.
No one remembers to ask anymore, they answer.
What do I expect in this New England seaport town, this birthplace of
    democracy,
Where I am a ghost?
Even a casino can't make an Indian real.
Or should I say "native," or "savage," or "demon"?
And with what rough language?
And then I am no longer in the dreaming mind but stepping off a train
From New York City.
Any earth language is a trade language.
I am trading a backwards look for jeopardy.
I agree with the ancient European maps.
There are monsters beyond imagination that troll the waters.
The Puritan's determined ships did fall off the edge of the world . . .
I am happy to smell the sea,
See the narrow winding streets of shops and restaurants, and delight
In the company of friends, trees, and small winds.
I want to have a good time, and would rather not speak with history
    over my plate of fish and catch up, but history came to me.
It's early and most of the men have left on a hunt from the Pequot vil-
    lage here; it's right here. Entrances are blocked and the village of
    women and children is set afire.
I do not want to know this.

Over six hundred are killed, to establish a home for God's people,
   crowed the Puritan leaders in their Sunday sermons.
And then history was gone in a betrayal of smoke.
And there is still burning though the walls are gone and we live in a
   democracy erected over the burial ground.
I am free to speak.
Every poem is an effort at ceremony.
I asked for a way in.

CHRISTOPHER MERRILL

All Hallows Eve

Dusk, and a gash of ochre bleeding through
The skin of the white pumpkin left in the patch
Given over to weeds, and husks of corn
Ground into the field harvested last night.
The costumed goblins running up the street
Aren't prepared for the first frost. The candle
Burning in the abandoned house casts shadows
Over the cabinets blackened with mildew.
The list of casualties taped to the wall
Outside the recreation center grows.

✦ ✦ ✦

The myth of innocence was what they cherished—
The noble lie that in their great republic
Nobody tortured prisoners of war,
Or monitored their lawyers' reading lists,
Or eavesdropped on a neighbor's conversation.
Easier to believe in ghosts—in the spirits
Of the original inhabitants
Of a land vouchsafed to them as in a dream
Of their benevolence, an occupation
Approved by all, or so they told themselves.

✦ ✦ ✦

The maze in which the rat and peacock slept
Through the tornado—rows of corn stalks spared
By an enterprising farmer who discovered

The joy of walking in a labyrinth
On Maui, on his second honeymoon,
In the parking lot of a small wooden church—
Alarms the guardsman's children who have come
On a Sunday school trip to the countryside
So that their mother can prepare the food
For the reception following the wake.

NATASHA TRETHEWEY

History Lesson

I am four in this photograph, standing
on a wide strip of Mississippi beach,
my hands on the flowered hips

of a bright bikini. My toes dig in,
curl around wet sand. The sun cuts
the rippling Gulf in flashes with each

tidal rush. Minnows dart at my feet
glinting like switchblades. I am alone
except for my grandmother, other side

of the camera, telling me how to pose.
It is 1970, two years after they opened
the rest of this beach to us,

forty years since the photograph
where she stood on a narrow plot
of sand marked colored, smiling,

her hands on the flowered hips
of a cotton meal-sack dress.

DAVID ST. JOHN

An Essay on Liberation

He stood naked at one of the two windows
She kept open in all weathers in her
Corner room at the back of the old building
As the sun rose   he watched a man
Dragging a handcart along the narrow alley below
& across the court a young boy was turning
His face from side to side in a freckled mirror
From the temples in the old section of the city
He could hear the first sequence
Of morning prayers   & to the west he could see
The dulled bronze domes of The Church of the Orthodox
Where at any moment the bells would begin to chime
& in the streets crisscrossing the city
From the old section to the sea
The tanks & personnel trucks began moving quietly
Into position in their orderly & routine way
& the bells began sounding from their tower
They were answered by the echoing concussion of mortars
As the daily shelling of the hills began
& she was slicing small pieces of bread the size of coins
To fry in goat butter & chives she was naked
Kneeling on one of the worn rugs thrown at angles across
The scarred floor   she glanced up at him & smiled
Nodding for no reason in particular   & in spite of
The fact the one phrase he'd taught her perfectly
Began with the world for *free*   though it ended
With *nothing*

KIM ADDONIZIO

November 11

2004

O everyone's dead and the rain today is marvelous!
I drive to the gym, the streets are slick,
everyone's using their wipers, people are walking
with their shoulders hunched, wearing hoods
or holding up umbrellas, of course, of course,
it's all to be expected—fantastic!
My mother's friend Annie, her funeral's today!
The writer Iris Chang, she just shot herself!
And Arafat, he's dead, too! The doctors refuse
to say what killed him, his wife is fighting
with the Palestinians over his millions, the parking lot
of the gym is filled with muddy puddles!
I run 4.3 m.p.h. on the treadmill, and they're dead
in Baghdad and Fallujah, Mosul and Samarra and Latifiya—
Nadia and Surayah, Nahla and Hoda and Noor,
their husbands and cousins and brothers—
dead in their own neighborhoods! Imagine!
Marine Staff Sgt. David G. Ries, 29, Clark, WA: killed!
Army Spc. Quoc Binh Tran, 26, Mission Viejo, CA: killed,
Army Spc. Bryan L. Freeman, 31, Lumberton, NJ same deal!
Marine Lance Cpl. Jeffrey Larn, 22, NY, you guessed it!
O I could go on and on, for as long as I live!
In Africa, too, they've been starved and macheted!
The morning paper said the Serbs apologized
for Srebrenica, 7,800 Muslims murdered in 1995,
I know it's old news, but hey, they're still dead!
I almost forgot my neighbor's niece, 16 and puking

in Kaiser Emergency, the cause a big mystery
until the autopsy—toxic shock syndrome,
of all things—I thought that was history, too,
but I guess girls are still dying; who knew! I run
for two miles, my knees hurt, and my shins,
I step off and stretch for a bit, I go back outside
into the rain, it feels chilly and good, it goes on
all day, unending and glorious, falling and filling
the roof-gutters, flooding the low-lying roads.

TONY BARNSTONE

Parable of the Jew without a Name

*"With our despised immigrant clothing, we shed also
our impossible Hebrew names."*
—Mary Antin, The Promised Land (1912)

My great-uncle Vincent, son of the Milk Street tailor,
threw some fairy dust into the air and changed,
making it easy for me to go to the prom,
to grow up in Indiana and bite my tongue
when a hick would cuss at *the bastard who tried
to Jew me down* on the price for homegrown pot.
Like wool pants for blue jeans, Moshe, Shmuel and Lazar
traded in their names, and in exchange were changed
from cabbage-eaters into Americans, and why not?
"I never was a pumpkin!," cries the carriage.
"I never was a pauper!," shouts the prince.
In this fairy tale all the steins turn into stones, straw turns
to gold, stars warp into crosses, and the pauper trades up
and leaves the trades to the star-crossed Jews.

I'm a lousy Jew, ignorant of nearly everything
except that in another time the Klan would lynch me,
the Nazis flay me into yellow lampshades.
My white hide hides me, my baseball cap keeps greasy ash
out of my hair, and I'm glad for my nice name.
Who needs a life so grim? In the shtetl, the old Jews
would change their names so the Angel of Death
flying on black crape wings above the town,
fatal list in hand, would pass over them
—but not the ones who stayed behind

and kept their names, the Adelsteins, Eisensteins
or the one I'll never know, some cousin twice removed
born in Poland, some Maurice Bernstein. No way to gather
smoke out of the sky and give him flesh again.

I imagine him, with eyes like mine, intent
and studious, staring at the rusted cattle-car wall
in the rattling stink of packed bodies, trying not to breathe.
He'll get that wish soon enough.
Slender, bookish children aren't good workers
and it's too much trouble to take away their names
and write numbers in their skin.
They're gassed like fleas.
I'm a lousy Jew, but I'd like to disturb the grass,
unearth him from the crowded grave, and let his damp fingers
write this story, while his eyes like clouded marble roll.
I'd like to roll the story back to the dead boy
swaying in the train, to see him there imagining the sky
he hasn't seen for days, the white winter sky, like a page
he could write on again and again, practicing his name.

MARILYN HACKER

Tahrir

Through the skein of years, I had nothing to fear from this place.
How final and brief it would be to disappear from this place.

The tangle of driftwood and Coke cans and kelp in the sand
made me think of the muddle that drove us (my dear) from this place.

An orchard, a vineyard, a stable, a river. A wall.
The impassable distance today once seemed simple and near from this
   place.

There was the word *refuge*, there was the word *refugee*
who, confused and disrupted, began to appear from this place.

The silence that lasted for decades, for months or for hours
will sooner or later be broken. You'll hear from this place.

There is a wall, and the words that we write on the wall,
Libertação! Can you make out *Tahrîr* from this place?

From your bedroom window with the sun coming up
I could see dusty jitneys crawl towards the frontier from this place.

My name's rhyme with yours and the things that are done in our
   names
in whatever writing no longer sound terribly clear from this place.

KIMIKO HAHN

Unrest

I saw the murder of Neda Agha-Soltan
en route to her underground singing lesson.

I saw the murder of Neda Agha-Soltan
barred from singing publicly, like all women.

Like all women,
I saw the murder of Neda Agha-Soltan.

I saw Neda Agha-Soltan
a sniper's bullet turning her from curious bystander to

Neda, *to voice* in Persian.

The dust in the cemetery is host
to protest against loss.

Neda Agha-Soltan, we all saw your murder,
after the rallies, the election, the counting.

Who counts, Neda Agha-Soltan?
Kimiko watched you die on a street in Tehran.

ANDREW HUDGINS

Summer of '09

For five miles, chanting *Stop the war*
and laughing with other laughters about
a government we almost trusted,
I did not wear black glasses
and a mask. No automatic rifle
swung up, muzzle firming from ellipse
to circle, assessing me, and I never,
black boots hammering my spine,
humped asphalt helplessly. At home,
sunburned, I cracked a beer,
not imagining the latch
shattering, rifle stock
clubbing the skull, military
heel planted on my back—fascism's
implacable penitentiary memes
of sadism and certitude. Last month,
in a prison uniform and thorazinic
monotone, I did not drone
my gratitude to the Brothers,
since purged, at the Intelligence Ministry
for awakening me to my errors.
My father was not summoned to receive,
in bloody, hardening sheets, my body—
each death and forced confession a scorched
tooth the dragon, in its madness,
wrenched from its roaring, necrotic jaw.

CHARLES HARPER WEBB

Reading about Rwanda

What if no morning newspaper flopped down beside the Welcome
    in front of my door?
What if my oatmeal box were empty; my orange juice pitcher, dry?
What if my solid brass faucets no longer flowed?

What if I turned the thermostat to Heat, and my furnace stayed cold?
What if I had no furnace—if the hinges had fallen off my doors,
    and the doors had been burned for firewood, and my house lay
    open to the hostile air?
What if I had no house?

What if the supermarket had no hamburger?
What if the Taco Bell had no tacos; the gas station, no gas, no air,
    no Gatorade in its refrigerated case?
What if all departments in department stores sold the same brand
    of Nothing?

What if there were no stores—just rubble that used to be walls?
What if armies, like waves in a trough, rolled back and forth
    across the country, killing everyone they saw?
What if the years of ease stopped like a movie—a romantic comedy—
    when the film burns through?

What if nobody was left to change the reel?
Then I would do, each dawn, the Dance of the Victim-in-Waiting,
    followed by the Dance of Spared-for-Now.
I would say the Prayer of So-Far-So-Good each night I survived.

However tired, before I slept I'd make the signs of Mayhem, and
    Kill Them Not Me.
Picking through rubble for food, I'd crack every rat bone,
        and smear my face with mud to show allegiance to Whoever
        Holds the Gun.
Those times I griped about traffic, sent back a steak, moped in bed
        because I wasn't more talented and loved,

Would fade until they seemed to happen in a mythic place
Where good people are rewarded with eternal peace,
Their loved ones greeting them with harps and kisses, no matter how
        their corpses look, or how they died.

DANA GIOIA

The Freeways Considered As Earth Gods

These are the gods who rule the golden land.
Their massive bodies stretch across the countryside,
Filling the valleys, climbing the hills, curving along the coast,
Crushing the earth from which they draw their sustenance
Of tar and concrete, asphalt, sand, and steel.

They are not new, these most ancient of divinities.
Our clamor woke them from the subdivided soil.
They rise to rule us, neither cruel nor kind,
But indifferent to our ephemeral humanity.
Their motives are unknowable and profound.

The gods do not condescend to our frailty.
They cleave our cities, push aside our homes,
Provide no place to walk or rest or gather.
The pathways of the gods are empty, flat, and hard.
They draw us to them, filling us with longing.

We do not fail to worship them. Each morning
Millions creep in slow procession on our pilgrimages.
We crave the dangerous power of their presence.
And they demand blood sacrifice, so we mount
Our daily holocaust on the blackened ground.

The gods command the hilltops and the valleys.
They rule the deserts and the howling wilderness.
They drink the rivers and clear the mountains in their way.
They consume the earth and the increase of the field.
They burn the air with their rage.

We are small. We are weak. We are mortal.
Ten thousand of us could not move one titan's arm.
We need their strength and speed.
We bend to their justice and authority.
These are the gods of California. Worship them.

STUART DISCHELL

The Squash Man

All these years living in the city, he still was not used to
Walking on concrete. In his province he went barefoot
With his sisters and chased the birds from the fields.
Their father grew squash and was known in the village
As the Squash Man. Their grandfather had been
The Squash Man too, at ease among the vines.

All these years living in the city and his feet still hurt him.
When the soldiers took him to war, they gave him boots
That did not fit. After the fields of the province were mined
By the soldiers and the crops rotted on their stalks
And grew moldy where the birds had picked them and his mother
Got shot by the soldiers for talking to the rebels and his father
Got shot by the rebels for talking to the soldiers, and his sisters
Escaped to the city where the police locked them in a brothel,
He spent his nights searching, his days washing dishes.

As far as he knew his ancestors had always lived on their land.
There was nowhere else they had known. In the city he lived
Outside in good weather and in abandoned factories in the rainy season.
There were too many streets in the city, too many shops and alleys.
He would never find his sisters or go back to the countryside.
He would never be the Squash Man. After the soldiers
Planted the mines, some farmers returned to their fields
Because they were starving. A joke went like this:
"What did the farmer say to his neighbor?"
"I would lend you a hand if I had one."

RICHARD KATROVAS

The Bridge of Intellectuals

If Crane had been a Czech, and deigned to live
Till '53, he might have more than praised
A bridge, for in that year of Stalin's death,
Artists and intellectuals of Prague—
But only those the Party had to fix
After an "elegant coup" in '48—
Finished their bridge across the Vltava.

Each morning did they bring their lunch in bags?
Did they bitch and curse and clown around behind
The foremen's backs? Were there foremen? Or did
Each man (were there women?) pull his weight
Unprodded by the ethos of his class?
Of eleven bridges down the spine of Prague
It stands the shabbiest and least necessary.
From the road leaving town one sees the tufts
Of grass and weeds muscling through the rusted
Transoms that trains, some say, must rarely cross,
And notes the webbed faults in the dark concrete
Of columns lifting from the water like
Wet khaki pant legs of old fishermen.
To those whose ambitions for bourgeois fame
Got them torn from their tasks to labor here,
Is there ironic consolation that,
As work is a matter of identity,
So many praised workers remain unnamed?

Anonymous bones of generations lie
The snaking length of China's ancient shyness;

Unknown apprentices applied the strokes
That smeared celestial radiance onto cheeks
Of lesser angels in the master works.

The petty, silly little men who snapped
The blossom of a generation from
Its living vine have watched their own bridge crumble,
And even as this bad joke stands unused,
Dilapidated on the edge of town,
Perhaps its "rehabilitated" builders—
Most dead by now, though some, no doubt, at work,
Scattered throughout Prague, in little flats, alone—
Feel vindicated in their bitterness,
If bitterness survives absurdity.

I'd like to know that once or twice a year
An old man, whose hands are soft from idle thought,
Comes, by bus or car, to gaze a while
And simply marvel that the thing still stands.

JORIE GRAHAM

Dialogue (Of the Imagination's Fear)

All around in
　　　　　houses near us, the
　　　　　layoffs,
　　　　　the windows shine back
　　　　　sky, it is a
　　　　　wonder we
can use the word *free* and have it mean anything at all
　　　　　to us. We stand still. Let the cold wind wrap round go
　　　　　into hair in-
between fingers. The *for sale* signs are bent and ripple in
　　　　　wind. One
had fallen last Fall and snowmelt is re-revealing
　　　　　it again. Rattle in groundwind. Siding
　　　　　weakening on
　　　　　everything. Spring!
　　　　　Underneath
　　　　　the bulbs want to clear the sill of
　　　　　dark and find the
　　　　　sun. I see
　　　　　them now
under there, in there, soggy with melt, and loam which is loosening as
their skins
rot, to let the whitest tendrils out, out they go snaking everywhere, till the
　　　　　leaves are blurring, they fur-out, they
　　　　　exist!—
　　　　　another's year loan
　　　　　to time—
and the bud will form in the sleeve of the silky leaf, and they will quietly,
among the slow working pigeons and there where a dog is leaping in
almost

complete invisibility, make slim heads,
thicken—I am ill, you know, says the man walking by,
his dog pulling him, so much joy, and nothing
will make it more or less, the flower,
as alive as it is dead, above which the girl with earphones walks humming,
no one
has warned her yet she is
free, but why, says the
imagination, have you sent me
down here, down among the roots, as they finally take
hold—it is hard—they wrench, the loam is not easy to open, I cannot
say it but the
smell is hope meeting terrifying regret, I would say do not open again,
do not go up,
stay under here there is
no epoch, we are
in something but it is not "the world," why try to make
us feel at
home down
here, take away the poem, take away this desire that
has you entering this waste dark space, there are not even pockets of
time here,
there are no mysteries, there is no laughter and nothing ever dies, the
foreclosure
you are standing beside look to it, there is a
woman crying on the second floor as she does not understand what it
will be like to
not have a home now, and how to explain to the children at 3:35 when
the bus drops
them off—
the root is breaking its face open and shoving up to escape
towards
sun—nothing can stop it—though right
now the repo-men have not yet come, the school bus is only just
getting loaded up,

the children pooling squealing some stare out the window. Kiss
              the soil as you
pass by. It is coming up to kiss you. Bend down to me, you have placed
me here, look
to me on all fours, drink of the puddle, look hard at the sky in there. It
is not sky. It is
              not there. The flame of
              sun which will come out just now for a blinding minute
into your eyes is saving nothing, no one, take your communion, your
blood is full of
              barren fields, they are the
              future in you you
              should learn to feel and
love: there will be no more: no more: not enough to go around; no
more around: no
              more: love that.

MICHAEL S. HARPER

Nelson Mandela's 90th Birthday ["Live in the Body, Long As You Will, Madiba"]

Qunu, South Africa: "one of the greatest figures of the 20th century."

I would dictate this to you by keeping my hands off the *secretary*
(no piece of furniture is a "secretary" in the British manor: she would
be alive)

I know only a little about imprisonment: 1962 at Pico Station: 11 11 '62
(*"Paradise Lost"* by John Milton with me; Book IV the devil's
kingdom, mine)

I gave up on the self at that interval; my brother in another cage—
same crime
(so little faith in self I thought three Indiana gangsters [white] were
worth insult)

I tried to put them in hell all-together
(meanwhile you sought justice for the whole world)

I tell you this in privacy of my own hell-hole
(trying to break out to repair & restore my soul in body)

I have met the solution: she is kind and smart: and can smell evil
(she tells me about "Alaska" and the Inuit: all in island-camps shrinking)

You know the 'Snow Lamp' *I speak of written by master-poet,*
Robert Hayden

(the discipline of life after death imprisoned in bad govt: our prophets of
space in song)

Somehow I will celebrate what you have earned in discipline
(she who somehow walks beside me will save all I have to give in your
world-view)

This is the praise poem in your Xhosa tradition
(she who will save me praises you as well)

NIKKI GIOVANNI

War Is Never Right

For some reason
Or perhaps
None
The dew was just lifting
Which is not unreasonable
But something for no reason
Made me walk
In my house slippers
To the little dogwood tree
Recently planted
By the shed

As I watered the tree
And, frankly, took joy
In the grass coming up
Where I had tried
for several years to no avail
to grow this little spot of green
I spotted a furry thing

Without thinking
I turned the hose on it
Assuming it was a mushroom
Or some of the mold
'That occasionally forms
On top of the mulch

I know there could not
Have been a scream because

Screams aren't possible
For little birds
But there was a protest

My heart broke

This little robin was out of the nest
Before she could fly
And I live with a Yorkie
Who was sniffing the yard

I grabbed the dog
Taking her back inside
And returned
To understand
This little bird would die

The mother was overhead now
And I put the bird in a basket
To take her beyond the reach
Of Alex though surely
Into the paw
Of one of the cats that roam

Some will say: *It's Mother Nature's
way* Some will say: *It's Natural*
Some will say: *It is out of your hands
There is **Nothing** you can do about it*

But it still breaks my heart
To know that little robin
Cannot be saved

DAVID MASON

Athena Looks On

"Back off this bitter skirmish;
end your bloodshed, Ithakans, and make peace."
—*Odyssey, Book XXIV (trans. Robert Fitzgerald)*

Athena looks on.
The whole earth is bruised.
Enough, enough.
My eyes are abused
by so much carnage.
Enough, enough.
It needs to be said.
The suicide bomb
in the afternoon
killed only beauty.
A husband alive,
a girl in her grief,
say, *Where is our Father?*
and where is relief?
Athena's gray eyes
have foreseen it all.
There is no surprise
that does not appall.
The child in your arms
is already dead.
Athena looks on,
looks on from a head
split open by birth,
spit open by death.
Athena looks on,

Athena looks on.
She looks on and on.
It needs to be said.

STANLEY MOSS

Jerusalem: Easter, Passover

1.

The first days of April in the fields—
a congregation of nameless green,
those with delicate faces have come
and the thorn and thistle,
trees in purple bloom,
some lifting broken branches.
After a rain the true believers:
cacti surrounded by yellow flowers,
green harps and solitary scholars.
By late afternoon a nation of flowers: Taioun,
the bitter sexual smell of Israel,
with its Arabic name, the flowering red clusters
they call *Blood of the Maccabees*,
the lilies of Saint Catherine, cool to touch,
beside a tree named *The Killing Father*,
with its thin red bark of testimony.
In the sand a face of rusted iron
has two missing eyes.

2.

There are not flowers enough to tell,
over heavy electronic gear
under the Arab-Israeli moon,
the words of those who see in the Dome of the Rock
a footprint of the Prophet's horse,
or hear the parallel reasoning
of King David's psalms and harp,
or touch the empty tomb.

It is beyond a wheat field to tell
Christ performed two miracles: first he rose,
and then he convinced many that he rose.
For the roadside cornflower
that is only what it is,
it is too much to answer
why the world is so, or so, or other.
It is beyond the reach
or craft of flowers to name
the plagues visited on Egypt,
or to bloom into saying why
at the Passover table Jews discard
a drop of wine for each plague, not to drink
the full glass of their enemy's suffering.
It is not enough to be carried off by the wind,
to feed the birds, and honey the bees.

3.

On this bright Easter morning
smelling of Arab bread,
what if God simply changed his mind
and called out into the city,
"Thou shalt not kill," and, like an angry father,
"I will not say it another time!"
They are praying too much in Jerusalem,
reading and praying beside street fires,
too much holy bread, leavened and unleavened,
the children kick a ball of fire,
play Islamic and Jewish games:
scissors cut paper, paper covers rock, rock breaks scissors.
I catch myself almost praying
for the first time in my life,
to a God I treat like a nettle
on my trouser cuff.

Let rock build houses,
writing cover paper, scissors cut suits.

4.

The wind and sunlight commingle
with the walls of Jerusalem,
are worked and reworked, are lifted up,
have spirit, are written,
while stones I pick up in the field
at random have almost no spirit,
are not written.

Is happiness a red ribbon on a white horse,
or the black Arabian stallion
I saw tethered in the courtyard of the old city?
What a relief to see someone repair
an old frying pan with a hammer,
anvil and charcoal fire, a utensil worth keeping.
God, why not keep us? Make me useful.

BILLY COLLINS

Boy Shooting at a Statue

It was late afternoon,
the beginning of winter, a light snow,
and I was the only one in the small park

to witness the lone boy running
in circles around the base of a bronze statue.
I could not read the carved name

of the statesman who loomed above,
one hand on his cold hip,
but as the boy ran, head down,

he would point a finger at the statue
and pull an imaginary trigger
imitating the sounds of rapid gunfire.

Evening thickened, the mercury sank,
but the boy kept running in the circle
of his footprints in the snow

shooting blindly into the air.
History will never find a way to end,
I thought, as I left the park by the north gate

and walked slowly home
returning to the station of my desk
where the sheets of paper I wrote on

were like pieces of glass
through which I could see
hundreds of dark birds circling in the sky below.

WILLIAM HEYEN

Angels

Years ago Dick Hugo wrote me to answer why
he'd cut out early from the White House reception
for poets—"too many angels there."

Jimmy Carter left his Oval Office for our reception line.
My wife & I followed Simic. When Charlie answered
"New Hampshire," our president's eyes brightened—

the "Live Free or Die" state's primary once mattered—
but then clouded again with the hostages in Tehran
who would cost him the next election. . . .

There were readings, we drank champagne.
We did not pose on a marble staircase for a photo.
Karl Shapiro said something rough & true for the papers,

& we all left this elegant wake for our homes
where we'd wonder what to do other than
trust to the underground tremors & voices of poetry.

Now many angels—James Wright, James Dickey, Hugo,
Gwendolyn Brooks, Ammons, May Swenson, Shapiro—
have died off who for one evening visited the powerless

residence of American power, but I'll remember
being with Han in one of the color-coded rooms.
Candleflame. A marine in dress blues standing

in shadows in each corner. Our pride. Our fear.
The crystal geometries of a chandelier.
A tall empire bookcase filled with leather wings.

SAM HAMILL

To Salah Al Hamdani, November, 2008

How many nights have I awakened, shocked,
my friend, at having dreamt of you again
as a young man learning to write poetry
in Abu Ghraib?

How many times have I invoked your name,
spoken of your exile, since that bright afternoon
five years ago when we met and embraced
on a stage in Piacenza, Italy?

I did not know your tongue, nor you mine,
but in our poetry we claimed fraternity,
solidarity in this alien world. Time
has not been kind to your beloved Baghdad.

Mutanabbi Street where you drank coffee
and searched the bookstalls long ago
has been bombed and bombed again.
The national library is no more.

You can bomb a bookstore or ban
a book, but it will not die. You cannot kill
a poem like you can a man.
Mutanabbi Street will rise again.

America will soon be led by a saner man.
The war in Iraq, for Americans, may end.
But for you and I and millions more,
exile doesn't end with the end of a war.

Five years ago we vowed to meet
one day on Mutanabbi Street,
and I hope that day will come.
But now it must be growing cold

and gray in Paris. In Buenos Aires,
summer is coming on, the great
acacias a canopy
over Palermo's narrow streets.

Sometimes I hear in the night
the clatter of hooves— horses
hitched to wagons, everything recycled—
and I am reminded: we too recycled,

we, too, are "known to horses,
to the wilderness and the night . . . "
But by no sword
will our brief song or enduring love survive.

MARY JO BANG

After the Fact

As if the world had four corners—in one, a war;
in another, a revolution against uninvited restrictions
on what one could think. In the third,

messages on microfilm tied to the ankles
of caged birds with teeth and talons pacing
and bickering about what "mine" means.

In the last, alone, someone dressed as the 21st Century,
skyscraper hat, flat-screen glasses,
stood at a table wondering about side effects

of medications and reward systems that are triggered
when boredom is bred in brains.
In a parable of panic and habit, a pilot landing

a crippled plane is like a country
where fearful rulers destroy dissent and whatever remains
goes from bad to worse. Sleep tight, you martyrs.

And you criminals who killed for a narrow share
of power and a few rotten spoils.
Enough is enough.

The corners converge, causing the globe to grow smaller
than all of time times space divided
by every petty difference.

The girl newly dead on the sidewalk says,
"Excuse me, but—
what kind of moral force is brute moral force?"

MARVIN BELL

The Book of the Dead Man (The Vote)

"Live as if you were already dead."
—Zen admonition

1. About the Dead Man and the Vote

The dead man was in the crowd when the militia moved in.

You can't know what the dead man who was there knows.

He was told to pipe down, to tread lightly, to wave when the leaders
passed on their way to the great hall.

He saw the past re-emerge from the future, he saw midnight at noon.

If a dead woman is walking on the street after an election and gets shot,
is that a vote?

And is beauty in the eye of the beholder, or shall we vote?

The candidate still wants to be in office when the Apocalypse comes.

The dead have voted, the injured have voted, those running from
the polling places have voted, and those awash in placards have
voted twice.

The dead man has voted with a pen, with a punch card, with a lever, in
ink and blood.

If there were more bread, we would not have to run through the sewers
clutching our ballots.

The dead man has seen the proud fingers of the illiterate, given a vote.

He has stood on line with the gerrymandered, the disenfranchised, the
ones who walked miles to make a mark, the hopeful and the fearful.

Shall the dead man choose among the old and new oppressors?

Shall he vote for the army, the navy, the palace guard, the elite, those
with the common touch, the new paradigm or the public statuary?

The dead man and woman will be sending absentee ballots.

They are the root and branch, the stem and the leaf of a free society.

2. More about the Dead Man and the Vote

The dead man keeps his powder dry, his lamp turned low, and his eyes
  on the sky.
He hears the say-so of change in the breeze, he sees the calligraphic
  dance of the reeds, he smells the dust where people ran.
The dead man will speak, and all the dead will speak, for you cannot
  soap the mouths of dead men and dead women.
He can smell a cleansing storm coming while there are ashes on
  his tongue.
The dead man has strung together the unlikely.
The despot never sees it coming, even as the voters throw open the
  palace doors.
Now the dead man sits down to a meal of rice and kebabs.
He could be talking to his beloved, to an engineer, to the ghost of
  Alexander the Great, it is a muttering under his breath.
The dead man hath disputed every election.
He hath counted the petitions and depositions, he hath tallied
  the ballots.
He hath seen the final figures approaching zero.
He hath placed a pox on the parties equally, on the candidates equally,
  on the party-line masses.
For it is only the independent for whom the dead man will vote.
The dead man does not buy and sell his preferences.
He enlists the chaos, he joins the rabble, he leads the caucus,
  then leaves.
The dead man is free.

CAROLYN FORCHÉ

The Museum of Stones

These are your stones, assembled in matchbox and tin,
collected from roadside, culvert and viaduct,
battlefield, threshing floor, basilica, abattoir—
stones, loosened by tanks in the streets
from a city whose earliest map was drawn in ink on linen,
schoolyard stones in the hand of a corpse,
pebble from Baudelaire's *oui,*
stone of the mind within us
carried from one silence to another
stone of cromlech and cairn, schist and shale, horneblende,
agate, marble, millstones, ruins of choirs and shipyards,
chalk, marl, mudstone from temples and tombs,
stone from the silvery grass near the scaffold,
stone from the tunnel lined with bones,
lava of a city's entombment,
chipped from lighthouse, cell wall, scriptorium,
paving stones from the hands of those who rose against the army,
stones where the bells had fallen, where the bridges were blown,
those that had flown through windows, weighted petitions,
feldspar, rose quartz, blueschist, gneiss and chert,
fragments of an abbey at dusk, sandstone toe
of a Buddha mortared at Bamiyan,
stone from the hill of three crosses and a crypt,
from a chimney where storks cried like human children,
stones newly fallen from stars, a stillness of stones, a heart,
altar and boundary stone, marker and vessel, first cast, load and hail,
bridge stones and others to pave and shut up with,
stone apple, stone basil, beech, berry, stone brake,
stone bramble, stone fern, lichen, liverwort, pippin and root,

concretion of the body, as blind as cold as deaf,
all earth a quarry, all life a labor, stone-faced, stone-drunk
with hope that this assemblage of rubble, taken together, would become
a shrine or holy place, an ossuary, immoveable and sacred
like the stone that marked the path of the sun as it entered the human
    dawn.

Rules Governing the Exchange of Prisoners

1.

As our representatives approach the border between our countries,
yours will simultaneously approach the border on your side.
After the agreed-upon recognition signals, the two groups
will come to a halt at a distance of fifty meters (translated to feet).

2.

It will be necessary at this stage to determine that the company
on either side consists of those previously and officially documented
and that no one is assuming an identity for the sake of espionage
or journalistic caprice. Neither side may bring along neutral observers.

3.

All utterance of friendly or hostile remarks will be discouraged
physically and forcefully, this not being an occasion for demonstrations
or arguments over who should have been made or called *prisoners*
or for contesting the relative merits or categories of national stereotypes.

4.

Both sides will then be subjected to thorough and intimate searches
by separate squads for photographs or written material or weapons
or books or money or valuables of any kind or foreign substances
or laundry, none of which will cross the border in either direction.

5.

The exchange itself will be a simple rearrangement of bodies.
Those presently in Country A will move under their own power

to Country B, and those presently in Country B will move by themselves
to Country A. At no time will the terms of this agreement be called
    into question.

6.

Individuals who are not prisoners but who take this occasion
to change sides and follow others under a different national banner
will be dealt with by the opposing authorities to be determined
mutually after bicameral collaboration or else shot.

Rules One through Six having been carried out to the letter,
those former prisoners still able to walk will assist the disabled
out of the dead zone in opposite directions not of their own choosing.
maintaining a disciplined silence and not looking back.

All the inconveniences of rehabilitation—the usual
unpatriotic language, repetitious behavior in the absence
of autism, the oversimplification of moral decisions,
tics, nightmares, catatonia—can be mitigated financially
and socially by the re-use of the protective facilities
previously devoted to the prisoners of the opposing nation.

ALICIA OSTRIKER

Language Acquisition: No and Yes

For the Refuser Network

At every moment somewhere in the world
some child is learning to say no
standing triumphant at the top of the stairs

or crying and turning red with frustration
at the parents: *I say no therefore I am
and you cannot stop me!*

Many possibilities sprout from this seed
this phoneme as powerful as zero
inside a person

a chromosome with a helmet on
and an optional comic mask—
Hitler and Stalin say *no,* the killer says a burning *no*

the suicide says *no,* but the poets
Moses Buddha Jesus Mohammed say *no and yes*
our friends in Cairo and Ramallah say *no and yes*

*no to the mind-forg'd manacles
no to the piggy palaces and cathedrals
yes to the page that says free yourself from mental slavery*

and the *yes* that springs from the deepest *no*
becomes a tree of life, fibers composed of words
its branches adorned with fruit of every shade

You cannot order me I refuse
You cannot order me I refuse

CHARLES BERNSTEIN

On Election Day

November 4, 2008

I hear democracy weep, on election day.
The streets are filled with brokered promise, on election day.
The miscreant's vote the same as saint's, on election day.
The dead unleash their fury, on election day.
My brother crushed in sorrow, on election day.
The sister does her washing, on election day.
Slowly, I approach the voices dark, on election day.
The men prepare for dying, on election day.
The morning hush defends its brood, on election day.
So still, so kindly faltering, on election day.
On election day, the cats take tea with the marmoset.
On election day, the mother refuses her milk.
On election day, the frogs croak so fiercely you would think that Mars
    had fallen into Earth.
On election day, the iron man meets her frozen gasp.
The air is putrid, red, interpolating, quixotic, torpid, vulnerable, on
    election day.
Your eyes slide, on election day.
Still the mourners mourn, the weepers wept, the children sleep alone in
    bed, on election day.
No doubt a comet came to see me, fiery and irreconciled, torrid,
    strummed, on election day.
On election day, the trespass of the fatuous alarm and ignominious
    aspiration fells the golden leap to girdled crest.
The tyrant becomes prince, on election day.
Neither friend nor foe, fear nor fate, on election day.
The liar lies with the lamb, on election day.

The last shall be the first and first sent to the back of the line, on
    election day.
The beggar made a king, on election day.
"Let him who is without my poems be assassinated!" on election day.
Let he who has not sinned, let him sin, on election day.
The ghosts wear suits, on election day.
On election day, sulfur smells like beer.
On election day, the minister quakes in fear.
On election day, the Pole and the Jew dance the foxtrot.
On election day, the shoe does not fit the foot, the bullet misfires in its
    pistol, the hungry waiter reels before steadying himself on facts.
The grid does not gird the fiddler, on election day.
Galoshes and tears, on election day.
The sperm cannot find the egg, on election day.
The drum beat becomes bird song, on election day.
I feel like a nightmare is ending but can't wake up, on election day.
on a shelf somewhere, and to hold it
for a better reason, if such should come, for it may.

CAROL FROST

Shoo

Crows settle on a fig bough and all grows
invisible until a caw falls from a yellow beak.
It's hard not to feel anger at the loud
assertion—like a demand for conquest
and God's revenge. Ironic, a murder
of crows eating fruit of paradise, every wild bite.
Shoo them so the figs might again be ours
and larks, once flown to sweet regions,
can return, flute by flute, freely to sing
from rooftops and gardens the songs
gotten by heart, part of our blood,
of Persian mountains and Persian moon.
Sometime between the century and the fig,
they'll return, after the crows have flown.

ROBERT WRIGLEY

Second Thoughts

"The flag, when it is in such condition that it is no longer
a fitting emblem for display, should be destroyed
in a dignified way, preferably by burning."
                                    —*US Code, Title 4, 8*

First of all, there is the matter of the tatters.
Such being the constancy of the winds
in these parts, this leeward edge over years
haggarded to a rickrack handsome fringe

is nevertheless close-up unraveled at least
an inch into its colonial symbolism.
And the sudden rains from the west
have, sadly, pinked its white at the dozen seams.

It is also old, the last two stars unadded
even half a century after the fact,
and the blue field by the sun has also been faded
to a day sky from the night's it is meant to represent.

Understand, I have burned flags before, tiny ones,
at least, favors from the cake at my going-away
party, when I was drafted, in 1971.
Though that seemed then, and still does today,

a better reason for burning than this is—
the tatters, the pinks, the palely faded blue—
so that among the possibilities of fittingness,
its age and wear do not move me to

do it, though I'd even contrived a kind of spit
to let it hang from, over a ceremonial fire,
this having struck me earlier as the sort of dignity
meant by the code's somber stricture.

Instead, I have decided to keep it, to fold it
in its traditional triangle and store it away

COLEMAN BARKS

Becoming Milton

Milton, the airport driver, retired now
from trucking, who ferried me
from the Greenville-Spartanburg airport
to Athens last Sunday midnight to 2:30 a.m.,
tells me about his son Tom, just back
from the Gulf War. "He's at Fort Stewart
with the 102nd Mechanized, the first tank unit
over the line, not a shot fired at them.
His job was to check the Iraqi tanks
that the airstrikes hit, hundreds of them.
The boy had never even come up on a car accident
here at home, twenty-four years old. Can you
imagine what he lifted the lid to find?
Three helmets with heads in them staring
from the floor, and that's just one tank.
He has screaming flashbacks, can't talk about it
anymore. I just told him to be strong
and put it out of his mind. With time,
if you stay strong, those things'll go away.
Or they'd find a bunker, one of those holes
they hid in, and yell something in American,
and wait a minute, and then roll grenades in
and check it and find nineteen freshly killed guys,
some sixty, some fourteen, real thin.
They were just too scared to move.
He feels pretty bad about it, truthfully,
all this yellow ribbon celebrating.
It wasn't a war really. I mean, he says
it was just piles and piles of their bodies.

Some of his friends got sick, started vomiting,
and had to be walked back to the rear.
Looks like to me it could have been worked
some other way. My boy came through OK,
but he won't go back, I'll tell you that.
He's getting out as soon as he can.
First chance comes, he'll be in Greenville
selling cars, or fixing them. He's good at both.
Pretty good carpenter too, you know how I know?
He'll tear the whole thing out if it's not right
and start over. There's some that'll look
at a board that's not flush and say *shit,*
nail it, but he can't do that, Tom."

TOM SLEIGH

World Cup

In all the cafes
on the seafront
whatever could be seen
kept exploding in riots

of blue, red, green—
horns everywhere hooting
for the ball soaring
toward the net.

Slicks of trash
and plastic glinting
from the waves, the world
was in a fever

to see the perfect goal,
the giant screens
on every corner
loud with the locust thrum

of satellite hookups.
Between two limestone cliffs
I plunged into the filth,
sucked a mouthful

of oil
and set out
swimming hard
to where I heard

rising voices
shouting in Arabic
Score Score.
A big wave swept

me under,
another and another,
until I shot out
of the water that gleamed

like a forehead butting mine,
expert but without malice
threatening to drag me down
until I slid out on the rocks.

I shivered, and wanted to live
in the clear light
of the announcers' voices
echoing in different languages

weaving a net so fine
the sun could pass through it—
yet you could see
in instant replay

the ball caught and caught
and caught, and not one stitch
of that fabric
going taut.

JEAN VALENTINE

In Prison

In prison
without being accused

or reach your family
or have a family   You have

conscience
heart trouble

asthma
manic depressive

(we lost the baby)
no meds

no one
no window

black water
nail-scratched walls

your pure face turned away
embarrassed

you
who the earth was for.

JAMES RAGAN

Now

For Neda Agha Soltan (1983–2009)

that the day's dead are numbered,
now that we work the bellows to fire up our will,
and the all-scarred children river out to remember
in succession that what they survive, a lie has killed,
Now that your father weeps on the long mast of a pillow
while at dawn the Basiji jogs, sleek as a lynx,
and the ragged claw in the Mullah's swallow
pulls back the gun's bowed sling, no one will think
how miseried your eyes for the gone-dead have grown,
how a nation shapes from the grave's felled quiet
the calm of your face in truth's carved stone.
How should we grieve for memory's delight
in our history's cruel blood lust,
should your voice rage to silence, water beading to dry dust?

NORMAN DUBIE

On the Ordination of a Zen Monk

For Chris

Basho is boiling his summer robes
beside a pond
with six red trees drowning in it —
his young friend is ripping
sides of flesh
off the steaming white catfish—
his knife still has the juice of apple on it.

Over the hill
court archers are at their new sport
of dog-killing. Basho has
immersed himself in the pond
but can still hear the peacocks
crying over the one wounded dog
who is running from the hunters
in the azure costumes.

When they find the poor animal
he is eating the earth, grinding his face into it
in an attempt to suffocate.
The archers mock the dog's suffering.

The weak leader in our *heike* senate
with a bad heart
shot a lawyer in the face
in dry standing corn—
there are

bits of white corn on his face
like fragments of human teeth.

The standing corn is a traditional refuge
for scrawny birds. The sleeves of the shocking corn
bleed as well. Basho cries to these hunters
who will shit rocks in hell
where time has no meaning and dogs
dispense mercy
to government officials and their wives
who also have lived lives that are cruel,

even brutal.

MAXINE KUMIN

Extraordinary Rendition

Only the oak and the beech hang onto their leaves
at the end, the oak leaves bruised the color of those
insurgent boys Iraqi policemen captured

purpling their eyes and cheekbones before
lining them up to testify to the Americans
that, no, no, they had not been beaten . . .

The beech leaves dry to brown, a palette of cinnamon.
They curl undefended, they have no stake in the outcome.
Art redeems us from time, it has been written.

Meanwhile we've exported stress positions, shackles,
dog attacks, sleep deprivation, waterboarding.
To rend: *to tear (one's garments or hair)*

in anguish or rage. To render: *to give what is due*
or owed. The pope's message
this Sunday is the spiritual value of suffering.

Extraordinary how the sun comes up
with its rendition of daybreak,
staining the sky with indifference.

DORIANNE LAUX

Staff Sgt. Metz

Metz is alive for now, standing in line
at the airport Starbucks in his camo gear
and buzz cut, his beautiful new
camel-colored suede boots. His hands
are thick-veined. The good blood
still flows through, given an extra surge
when he slurps his latte, a fleck of foam
caught on his bottom lip.

I can see into the channel in his right ear,
a narrow darkness spiraling deep inside his head
toward the place of dreaming and fractions,
ponds of quiet thought.

In the sixties my brother left for Vietnam,
a war no one understood, and I hated him for it.
When my boyfriend was drafted I made a vow
to write a letter every day, and then broke it.
I was a girl torn between love and the idea of love.
I burned their letters in the metal trash bin
behind the broken fence. It was the summer of love
and I wore nothing under my cotton vest,
my Mexican skirt.

I see Metz later, outside baggage claim,
hunched over a cigarette, mumbling
into his cell phone. He's more real to me now
than my brother was to me then, his big eyes

darting from car to car as they pass.
I watch him whisper into his hands.

I don't believe in anything anymore:
god, country, money or love.
All that matters to me now
is his life, the body so perfectly made,
mysterious in its workings, its oiled
and moving parts, the whole of him
standing up and raising one arm

to hail a bus, his legs pulling him forward,
all muscle and sinew and living gristle,
the countless bones of his foot trapped in his boot,
stepping off the red curb.

CAROL MUSKE-DUKES

Ex-Embassy

Sometimes, near dawn, I think I hear the high
sobbing cry of the muezzin hanging in the sky
before it's light—but then, I drop off to sleep again.

Behind us is the ex-embassy.
Its pool a blue mosaic through
our hedge. The old man in his
robe and wrapped head no longer

comes to mop the tiled edge,
his whole morning's work
fragmented by our wall of leaves.
No arm in a rolled sleeve,

bending, lifting. No flashing sections
of aluminum pole fit into a blue mesh
scoop to whisk up floating red petals.
No closer view, inset in green:

a turbaned man sipping tea,
eyebrow and striped cup;
slice of a woman's profile—
black half-veil, two eyes

yoked in kohl moving in a
handheld mirror. No sunlight
gunning that round of glass. No part
of lamb turning on part of a spit.

No peacock with its promiscuous fan.
No cook hurrying the meat: quick jagged
curses. No meat. No god. The medallion
frontispiece now defaced officially,
                    the cornices deflagged,
but still the scarred remnants of State:
crude evidence of our power to invade,
theirs to resist.

     The FOR SALE sign's text
likens it to a house on a cloud,
a secular mosque, pure sunrise!
There are patterned entry tiles:

repeating fronds of wheat or hashish.
A *porte cochere*, nesting rotating
motion detectors. Double, triple glass.

Once a prying neighbor said she
heard grown men cry out, in
a frenzy, on a stone floor—
to some god she fails to
comprehend. No one, she says,
(over the hedge on the other side)

comprehends that god. Because,
like the one in the rubbed lamp,
once out, uncramped,
          he's *not*.

He's not anything or anyone you
could imagine, beyond the figuration of
your own god, the familiar reductive Infinite.

For her, this deity is zero, spun from Os of fuel
drums, snaking wires. He's rolled up in a child's valise,
genie of timing devices, threads of plastique . . .

I don't see the nothing she does. Sometimes I glimpse
an imagined Allah above the human ruins,
head in hand. Then I watch my own fingers, telling

each invisible worry bead of each amber hour
that we all stay alive. Inside each separate sphere,
the lights of patrols slip by, elongating a single night,

    then the next, the next . . .

                    what I do not know
                    but learn to dread
                    turns over slowly in my bed.

MAXINE HONG KINGSTON

August 6, and again on August 9

The people on the far shore
slid rows of lanterns upon the water
on careful ramps
nudged them

    go   go

The paper and the tiny flames shook

    no no   no no

We willed them (replicas of lives)—
Blow downstream toward the setting sun.
But the wind breathed them
to our side of the water,
where nodding, turning,
they shyly touched
one another.

"There's mine!"
A little girl sees her writing:

    No More Bombs
    On Hiroshima
    On Nagasaki
    On Pearl Harbor
    On Iraq
    On NY City

A loudspeaker
calls lost children. "Jonathan,
your mother's looking for you."
A man in a wheelchair zooms across
the bridge, sailing an American flag.

QUINCY TROUPE

The Allusion of Seduction

even when you sat in the glowing embers
during that day as any other, the sun,
sinking quickly as the breath of a dying man,
who felt the light dimming in his sunken eyes,
lingered, as the sweet touch of a woman's lips
you loved, lingered, like a cool breeze on your flesh
after she left, her perfume hanging in the air there
like seduction, you remembered her incredible tongue
licking so softly, so feathery-light across your keening body,
was so electric then, is so electric now in your memory,
as this moment is electric when you feel
the beauty of language growing inside a poem,
inside the incredible music of its reference,

on the other hand it is a different moment now
under this black sky filled with stars silent as people
walking around down here imitating zombies,
where you sit, sifting through the wreckage of memory
you hear voices swelling from somewhere deep within
hidden crevices of an invisible stillness,
a plunging hush where once there was a clamoring,

a nervous cacophony filled with agitation, were marching
people around the globe speaking in one voice,
waving banners, thrusting fists—of all colors—
into the glowing air like pistons, when the light dropped over
the edge of the world during a sunset you remember, when
the police surged forward wearing gas masks,
they looked like darth vaders swinging steel batons,
cracking human skulls as if they were piñatas

& hidden behind their sparta shields made people dance
when they shot them with garrulous, voluble water hose's,
in the glowing light dropping over the edge of the world
at sunset, in this moment here, this eerie silence
the presence comes rushing at you with the urgency
of that garrulous water hose, drowning out all nostalgia,

& you think of guantanamo, guantanamo, O the shame,
of guantanamo, abu ghraib, the silence,
the creeping national silence of voices ignoring the known,
the cold-blooded depravity of it all, the insulation

we freeze ourselves into so we won't recognize
the horror in front of us, so familiar
as apple pie, the graphic scenes of a tarantino movie,
the impoverishment of spirit we find located
inside ourselves, we have no language that speaks

& yet you remember still the sweetness of her lips
brushing over your flesh like feathers of a bird's wing,
her incredible licking tongue lathering
your body with its honey, its seduction of your keening body
made so electric by her touch, her wondrous perfume
hanging in the air like beautiful language inside a poem
& you linger over the memory of all of this,
feel hope is still there, as long as there is love

JUAN FELIPE HERRERA

Dear Prudence

Towers rumbled & gassed down
Missiles gnawed & sawed down
The dictators transferred out of this moment-world

Severed money sky-scrapered up
Ancient oil & the bank shooting blood across the fiber grid

We walk the darkness the hunger streets
Fire fountains fire oceans we idle at the gate
We bow down before the ignited world

GERALD STERN

Asphodel

He was dead so he was only a puff
of smoke at the most and I had to labor to see him
or just to hear and when we spoke it was as
if we were waiting in the rain together
or in a shelter on 96th street or by the
side of a train in Washington, D.C., say,
changing engines and patting each others' stomachs
by way of intimacy, and he said what he
wanted most of all, when it came to trains,
was merely to stand on the platform looking out
the dirty window at the water beyond
the row of houses or the stand of trees
for it was *distance* he loved now and the smell of
the ocean, even more than coffee, but it was
only *concoction* for he didn't have the senses
anymore and I forgot to say that
he was a veteran and he wore a green cap
that had "Korea Veteran" printed on the face
with three bright battle ribbons below the lettering,
and I forgot to say his ears were large,
the way it sometimes happens in older men,
though he was dead, and he was on the train with
his wife who had red hair of sorts and a dress
that spread out like a tassel of silk, and war
was what we talked about and what the flowers
were the way a poppy was the emblem
of World War One and we both laughed at how
there were no flowers for Korea nor any
poems for that matter though he was sad and although

he wore the hat he said it was a stupid
useless war, unlike Achilles Odysseus
talked to in Hell, who loved his war and treasured
the noses he severed and the livers he ruptured,
and picture them selling their asphodel in front of
a supermarket or a neighborhood bank
and picture us waiting until our ears were long
just to hate just one of their dumb butcheries.

Dark Thirty

All year, death, after death, after death.
Then today look how majestically clouds float in the sky,
God putting on a show of tenderness, nothing like thoughts
that rise and drift in my mind, like the flakes shaken
in a snow globe, and my brain laboring in its own night,
never feeling the punky starlight of dark thirty, the time
a friend said for us to meet and had to explain it was half an hour
after the first dark, when day lilies fold up and headlights
lead the way home, but maybe too early
to find the moon turning half its body away,
holding it hidden like the black side of a mirror, unseen
until it breaks, unexpectedly, the way grief
breaks over you when you've already given all you've got
and hands you tools you don't know how to use.

The blush of dark thirty turned bleak
when I heard about the O—
O dark thirty, military time for 12:30 a.m.,
hour of the deepest dark, when, if I'm awake,
as I often am, a storm of thoughts battles one another, now settling
unsettlingly on the ways we make war and flaunt it.
Take the Civil War–era double cannon on the lawn
of a city hall in the deep south, twinned so that two cannonballs
chained together kill two at a time, often decapitating.
And why did a small town, population 932, in rural New Hampshire,
import a ballistic missile to crown its village green?

Brecht's line floats up: "Pity the nation that needs heroes,"
but what to do with the guy pontificating on the Middle East,

telling me with the gravest authority—
that of stupidity—the reason for the strife there:
"Hatred is in the rocks."

Teacup Manifesto

Bivouacked in a woman's living room,
a heap of soldiers, dusty as flour sacks,
sleeps on her carpet. Will the woman ever
return to beat those crimson fibers free of their
sifting particles? The slanted teacup tower
in her cabinet behind them must tremble
every time a soldier groans or turns.
The ridged wool of the carpet against their cheeks
makes creases they'll have to rub from their faces,
when they tear off the webs of sleep.
Probably none of the teacups will survive.
The boys gloves look so thick they might
not even be able to pick one up
without taking the mitts off first.
The teacups slightly gasp from the seepage of dust.

Long, long from January 18, 2007, and
the photograph I have tumbled into, in
a hypnogogic moment between sleep,
the new cats' cries, and the filling of the teakettle,
I imagine a museum case unlocked,
and a twisted fiber from her carpet, labeled
and numbered, laid next to a classified shard
(one of her cups). From this someone
will be obliged to imagine an entire civilization.
Armpit rot, crotch rot, and the rank smell of sleep
let the boys steep the tea of their dreams,

while my husband, so much older than these kids,
lies drenched in a fever, curled up in our bed
and, in the boundary-less anxiety of the kettle steam,
I worry equally about the lost woman not
on the cover of the newspaper, and him,
and the boys. The still photo comes alive
and they thrash, raw, curling into each other
as my husband curls—and as the metal
cocking of the cat food can brings
the animals to swarm their saucers,
I cleave to the unformed idea that
it must be cups men fight for.
The chance to wake in a sweat and drink
from something that claims a moment of peace
just because it could break.

SHARON DOUBIAGO

Fatwa

"Writing itself is one of the great, free human activities."
—William Stafford

I saw you in Café Roma the day after Thanksgiving writing in your
    notebook.
You sat at the little table in the window among students at their
    laptops, your regal head

lifted slightly as if above the burnt coffee aroma, your pen poised to the
    six-by-nine, wire-bound tablet
for the next word

which may take awhile. I was standing in the line weighted with
    revelations of my family
newly discovered in my writing, stunned

to see you, the Nobel Prize winner for literature, sentenced to death—
    the fatwa for fiction!—writing
so visibly in this noisy public place, your assassin guaranteed his or her
    place in Heaven.

I could see across the room the neatness of your lines, the
    deliberateness with which you set
down each letter. I didn't know the language you were writing but I
    know writers who won't advance

one word until they have the right one. Myself I could not release a
    single syllable
if I called the guards to the gates first. I fly over to where I'm burning

come back later for the imprisoned. Opening to the self,
allowing others however foreign to open to their selves, is the rule of
   writing.

I was experiencing the immense privilege of seeing the trance the
   famous writer was in
when your shining eyes flashed into mine.

I turned away. A minute later I turned back. You were still staring at
   me. I was sorry
to recognize you—recognized, you're in danger – sorry to rob you of
   your meditation.

I worked not to look again. The thought did cross my mind, but no
   way could you recognize me
though conceivably you saw the writer, survivor too, her mind, her
   father always charged

working overtime. Or maybe, your eyes beaming directly on me were
   not seeing me at all
other than as one watches for an assassin in any crowd.

Your clothes were rich beiges, golds and ivories, your vest and rolled-up
   sleeves, your gold sock
onto the shining shoe crossed over the left leg the same as your gold-
   streaked, brown curly locks

and glowing skin just from the sauna, your eyes over the gold rims
   staring at me in my rags.
Behind you outside on the corner a homeless boy was selling his rag for
   a dollar. Suddenly

borne across your left manicured shoulder your translator came out of
   the concert in Tokyo
got in his VW and turned on the key

FATWA! Jesus
was executed for blasphemy too. Joan of Arc for wearing men's clothing.

It's issued at our birth to block all word of what goes on inside the
    castle walls.
In our innocence we honor this. The sacred duty

of the lover is to protect the privacy of the loved ones but I wrote a story
from their dictation not realizing their lies. I vowed never again.

Years I wouldn't write, years their fear increased. They assassinated my
    character
in case their fatwa failed

so that whatever might appear would not be believed. They knew
what they had silenced, a song about whales

rising from another story my sister told me years ago, just a fragment
in a small sweet poem, but now so rooted in me I breathe it in and out
    as fact, my flesh

singing it on a stage in a new city so that a young man in the audience
recognized the long-dead whale scholar who'd written the text,
    recognized her lover.

Only then did I read it through the tyranny of her lies, did I ponder his
    wife and children.
Not to write of my sister is not to write of myself. You or Earth.

Not to write my self, my story is not to know it. Is not to live it. Is to
    live my life
created by their lies, by order of the State that will not know the poet.

The condemned, but living, famous writer was still staring at me, your
   pen still stopped
on the page, your mind overtime in the caffeine and car exhaust ozone.
   You had a wife

a writer too who hid with you. The announcement of her leaving you
   screamed around the world.
I hoped she was going out as counter and shield to pave the way, the
   divorce

a lie to throw the killers off, a strategy, for your survival, and to protect
   her too.
From the whale song inside me I know a million fatwas could not have
   torn me from my husband then.

And now running in from the street across your right shoulder Pacific
   salmon were flying
up the river mouths, flying over the dams and the unknown poet in
   her rags

about to write

> *for Salmon Rushdie, Berkeley, November 2002*

What's Fair Is Fair

The police didn't do anything to them. Legs in stockings

with flowers. Windows and plants. The potting shed. Some children
have to run away in the middle of the night

to join the circus. Some people stand around forever it seems alongside
the airport conveyor belt. Here in the tissue paper

silence and sunlight flap their wings.

The god who wanted to be a truck driver

takes out a fruit stand. He knows what you're thinking. The traffic's
bad. Take the money

bunny. What are you wearing.

The weather's old and personal. It doesn't

have an end. That's

the bottom line.

CHRISTOPHER BUCKLEY

Poverty

"la colera de pobre
tiene dos rios contra muchos mares."
—Cesar Vallejo

Vallejo wrote that with God we are all orphans.
I send $22 a month to a kid in Ecuador
so starvation keeps moving on its bony burro
past his door—no cars, computers,
basketball shoes—not a bottle cap
of hope for the life ahead . . . just enough
to keep hunger shuffling by in a low cloud
of flies. It's the least I can do,
and so I do it.
                    I have followed the dry length
of Mission Creek to the sea and forgotten to pray
for the creosote, the blue salvia, let alone
for pork bellies, soy bean futures.
                              Listen.
There are 900 thousand Avon Ladies in Brazil.
Billions are spent each year on beauty products
world-wide—28 billion on hair care, 14 on skin
conditioners, despite children digging on the dumps,
selling their kidneys, anything that is briefly theirs.
9 billion a month for war in Iraq, a chicken bone
for foreign aid.
                    I am the prince of small potatoes,
I deny them nothing who come to me beseeching
the crusts I have to give. I have no grounds for complaint,
though deep down, where it's anyone's guess,

I covet everything that goes along with the illustrious—
creased pants as I stroll down the glittering boulevard,
a little aperitif beneath Italian pines. But who cares
what I wear, or drink? The rain? No, the rain is something
we share—it devours the beginning and the end.

The old stars tumble out of their bleak rooms like dice—
Box Cars, Snake Eyes, And-The-Horse-You-Rode-In-On . . .
not one metaphorical bread crumb in tow.
Not a single *Slaudo!* from the patronizers
of the working class—Pharaoh Oil, Congress,
or The Commissioner of Baseball—all who will eventually
take the same trolley car to hell, or a slag heap
on the outskirts of Cleveland.
                                         I have an ATM card,
AAA *Plus* card. I can get cash from machines, be towed
20 miles to a service station. Where do I get off penciling in
disillusionment? My bones are as worthless as the next guy's
against the stars, against the time it takes light to expend
its currency across the cosmic vault. I have what everyone has—
the over-drawn statement of the air, my blood newly rich
with oxygen before the inescapable proscenium of the dark,
my breath going out equally with any atom of weariness
or joy, each one of which is closer to God than I.

PHILIP LEVINE

The Gatekeeper's Children

This is the house of the very rich.
You can tell because it's taken all
The colors and left only the spaces
Between colors where the absence
Of rage and hunger survives. If you could
Get close you could touch the embers
Of red, the tiny beaks of yellow,
That jab back, the sacred blue that mimics
The color of heaven. Behind the house
The children digging in the flower beds
Have been out there since dawn waiting
To be called in for hot chocolate or tea
Or the remnants of meals. No one can see
Them, even though children are meant
To be seen, and these are good kids
Who go on working in silence.
They're called the gatekeeper's children,
Though there is no gate nor—of course—
Any gatekeeper, but if there were
These would be his, the seven of them,
Heads bowed, knifing the earth. Is that rain,
Snow or what smearing their vision?
Remember, in the beginning they agreed
To accept a sky that answered nothing,
They agreed to lower their eyes, to accept
The gifts the hard ground hoarded.
Even though they were only children
They agreed to draw no more breath
Than fire requires and yet never to burn.

CARL DENNIS

More Poetry

When he read of a woman in a village
Fifty miles south of Teheran
Teaching English to her high-school class
By teaching Whitman, my friend Herbert
Decided to lead an online discussion group
On Iranian poetry. True, he knew little
About the subject; but having been moved
By her conviction that it's hard to spurn
A nation when you know its poets,
He wanted to make the subject his own.

Ignorant, yes, but prompt to admit it
And invite those who knew more
To be generous, once a week, with suggestions;
Grateful if someone helped with a stubborn passage
By offering a translation truer to the original
Than the one in the book he'd chosen.
What seemed to be a boulder blocking the path
Suddenly proves a bush whose comely flowers
Travelers pause awhile to admire
Before they step around it and move on.

Two hours of steady progress,
And then, when he turns from the screen,
An hour of imagining what went on
Today in the village classroom.
"Can anyone tell me," he can hear the woman asking,
"What the word *limitless* means in Whitman's lines,
'Limitless are leaves stiff or drooping in the fields

And brown ants in the little wells beneath them'?
Is he saying simply 'too many to count'
Or something bolder and farther-reaching?"

And if some students conclude it means "priceless"
To those who are free enough to see
The low as lofty, the last as first,
While others are sure it means "wholly beyond
Our limited human understanding,"
She doesn't push for consensus.
"Whitman would likely be happy," she tells them,
"With either answer. But to take the two
As two twigs leafing out on a tree
Outside our window might please him more."

THOMAS LUX

The People of the Other Village

hate the people of this village
and would nail our hats
to our heads for refusing in their presence to remove them
or staple our hands to our foreheads
for refusing to salute them
if we did not hurt them first: mail them packages of rats,
mix their flour at night with broken glass.
We do this, they do that.
They peel the larynx from one of our brothers' throats.
We devein one of their sisters.
The quicksand pits they built were good.
Our amputation teams were better.
We trained some birds to steal their wheat.
They sent to us exploding ambassadors of peace.
They do this, we do that.
We canceled our sheep imports.
They no longer bought our blankets.
We mocked their greatest poet
and when that had no effect
we parodied the way they dance
which did cause pain, so they, in turn, said our God
was leprous, hairless.
We do this, they do that.
Ten thousand (10,000) years, ten thousand
(10,000) brutal, beautiful years.

GALWAY KINNELL

Wait

Wait, for now.
Distrust everything if you have to.
But trust the hours. Haven't they
carried you everywhere, up to now?
Personal events will become interesting again.
Hair will become interesting.
Pain will become interesting.
Buds that open out of season will become interesting.
Second-hand gloves will become lovely again;
their memories are what give them
the need for other hands. The desolation
of lovers is the same: that enormous emptiness
carved out of such tiny beings as we are
asks to be filled; the need
for the new love *is* faithfulness to the old.

Wait.
Don't go too early.
You're tired. But everyone's tired.
But no one is tired enough.
Only wait a little and listen:
music of hair,
music of pain,
music of looms weaving our loves again.
Be there to hear it, it will be the only time.

Afterword

I Didn't Ask For My Parents

It isn't like you bend
your dainty spirit neck
down from God's baby-soul-land
and point to a copulating couple
who strike your fancy.

Don't think it works that way.

You are blind-folded
and shot down through heaven's tunnel
into life and where you plop
willy-nilly that's your home.

The Jewish couple may be in the act
at the same time as their Muslim neighbor.

Where you end up
even the cherub who pushed you off
the edge can't know.

We grow up forgetting
our incidental placements
become fond of whatever
bread and religion we are fed.

Listen,

Who has salvation
when we all claim it?

Sholeh Wolpé

Acknowledgments

Sholeh Wolpé and PEN Center USA wish to express their gratitude to the poets in this anthology for gifting their poems to this project. We also thank and acknowledge the following publications in which some of the poems in this collection have appeared:

Ex-Embassy, from *Applause,* by Carol Muske-Dukes, University of Pittsburgh Press, 1989. Copyright © by Carol Muske-Dukes. Used by permission of the author. *Reading About Rwanda,* from *Tulip Farms and Leper Colonies,* by Charles Harper Webb, BOA Editions, Ltd, 2001. Copyright © by Charles Harper Webb. Used by permission of the author. *Angels* by William Heyen, first appeared as *Wings* in *Ribbons: The Gulf War,* Time Being Books, 1991. Copyright © by William Heyen. Used by permission of the author. *The Book of the Dead Man (The Vote),* from *Vertigo: The Living Dead Man Poems,* by Marvin Bell, Copper Canyon Press, 2011. Copyright © by Marvin Bell. Used by permission of the author. *Becoming Milton,* from *Winter Sky, New and Selected Poems, 1968–2008,* by Coleman Barks, University of Georgia Press, 2008. Copyright © by Coleman Barks. Used by permission of the author. *Now,* from *The World Shouldering I,* by James Ragan, Salmon Poetry Publishing, 2012. Copyright © by James Ragan. Used by permission of the author. *The Allusion of Seduction* from *Errancities,* by Quincy Troupe, Coffee House Press, 2012. Copyright © by Quincy Troupe. Used by permission of the author. *The Museum of Stones* by Carolyn Forché was first published in The New Yorker, March, 26, 2007. Copyright © by Carolyn Forché. Used by permission of the author. *An Essay on Liberation,* from *Study For the World's Body,* by David St. John, Harper Collins, 1994. Copyright © by David St. John. Used by permission of the author. *November 11,* from *Lucifer at the Starlite,* by Kim Addonizio, W. W. Norton, 2009. Copyright © by Kim Addonizio. Used by permission of the author. *Tahrir,* by Marilyn Hacker, from *Saudad: an anthology of Fado poetry,* edited by Mimi Khalvati, Clouste Gulbenkian Foundation, 2010. Copyright © by Marilyn Hacker. Used by permission of the author. *Teacup Manifesto,* from *The Second Blush,* by Molly Peacock, W. W. Norton Co, 2009.

Sholeh Wolpé, from *The Scar Saloon*, Red Hen Press, 2004. Copyright © by Sholeh Wolpé. Used by permission of the author. *Call and Answer*, by Robert Bly, from *The Insanity of Empires*, Ally Press, 2004. Copyright © by Robert Bly. Used by permission of the author. *End of the War, 1949*, by Willis Barnstone, from *Algebra of Night: Selected Poems, 1948–1998*, Sheep Meadow Press, 1998. Copyright © by Willis Barnstone. Used by permission of the author. *Dialogue (Of The Imagination's Fear)*, by Jorie Graham, from *Place*, Ecco, 2012. Copyright © by Jorie Graham. Used by permission of the author. *History Lesson*, by Natasha Trethewey, from *Domestic Work.*, Graywolf Press, 2000. Copyright © by Natasha Tretheway. Used by permission of the author. *Staff Sgt. Metz*, by Dorianne Laux, from *The Book of Men*, W. W. Norton, 2011, Copyright © by Dorianne Laux. Used by permission of the author. *Night in Blue*, by Brian Turner, from *Here, Bullet*, Alice James Books, 2005. Copyright © by Brian Turner. Reprinted with the permission of the Alice James Books, and BLOOD-AXE Books LDT (U.K.) *Wait*, by Galway Kinnell, from *Mortal Acts, Mortal Words*, Houghton Mifflin Company, 1980. Copyright © by Galway Kinnell. Used by permission of the author. *World Cup*, by Tom Sleigh, from *Five Points*, Georgia State University, 2011. Copyright © by Tom Sleigh. Used by permission of the author. *Dark Thirty*, by Barbara Ras, from *The Last Skin*, Penguin, 2010. Copyright © by Barbara Ras. Used by the permission of the author. Reprinted with the permission of Penguin, a division of Penguin Group (USA) Inc *Kubota to Miguel Hernandez in Heaven, Leupp, Arizona, 1942*, by Garrett Hongo, from *Coral Road*, Knopf, 2011. Copyright © by Garrett Hongo. Used by the permission of the author. Reprinted with the permission of Alfred A. Knopf, a division of Random House, Inc..

Notes

"November 11" by Kim Addonizio

The first time I visited the Wall, the Vietnam veterans memorial in Washington, I was overwhelmed by the power of all those names, each name a life lost. But each name also a life honored and remembered. I think that's one impulse of poetry: to name what passes, trying to hold it in our hearts a little longer.

The opening line of "November 11" came into my head on Veterans Day in 2004 complete with that grandiose "O" and exclamation point. I was driving to the gym, thinking what I have often thought: "Wow, it's all creation and destruction at the same time, every moment." As I was working on the poem and started naming, I found I didn't want to stop. I wanted to fix those people in memory. But I soon saw what an impossible task that was; there were—are—too many dead. That's partly what the poem is about. The rain is for me the astonishing dailiness of all this death, so much of it from war and violence.

I used some Iraqi women's names because that's what I thought about, the women there who were dying and losing their loved ones. And the four American soldiers were listed in the *San Francisco Chronicle* that day, part of the ongoing body count. The exclamation points are meant to be both sincere and ironic, just as the rain becomes both the beauty of being alive and the continuation of all of our forms of ignorance.

"To Salah Al Hamdani, November, 2008" by Sam Hamill

Salah Al Hamdani is an Iraqi poet/actor who's lived in exile in Paris for the last thirty years. He learned to write poetry while in Saddam's Abu Ghraib.

"Language Acquisition: No and Yes" Alicia Ostriker

The Refuser Solidarity Network (RFN) was formed in Israel in 2002, triggered by a public letter signed by fifty-two Israel Defense Forces reserve officers refusing military service in the Occupied Territories. The overall objective of the RFN is to support Israeli citizens who refuse to serve the Occupation.

"Ex-Embassy" by Carol Muske-Dukes
For twenty years I lived in a beautiful house in Hancock Park on
Windsor Square in Los Angeles, and just beyond our backyard, the
next street over, was the embassy of a Middle Eastern country. The
embassy was there for many years, but the official residents were quiet
and very private and rarely seen. Sometime before September 11, 2001,
the embassy was officially closed and vacated, and all remnants of its
diplomatic mission status were erased, sort of. Sconce-like flag-holders,
the imprint of the official embassy seal, could still be seen even after
power-washing and repainting. The ghost of the ambassador remained
in residence, even as the house went up for sale. The ex-embassy is an
obvious metaphor, in my poem, for the cultural distrust and fear that
fuels our relationship to the Middle East, from the individual's terror of
Terror to the highest state refusal of diplomatic solutions and dialogue.

"Fatwa" by Sharon Doubiago
Hitoshi Igarashi, Salmon Rushdie's Japanese translator of *The Satanic
Verses,* was stabbed to death outside his Tokyo university office in July
1991. The poem is what I saw. There have been many fire bombings,
injuries, and deaths as a result of this fatwa; I have a memory of reading
of the incident as I describe.

"More Poetry" by Carl Dennis
Though many great poems have been written in countries that were
not democracies—that were, at times, radical tyrannies—a link does
exist between a love of poetry and the tolerance of diversity, for poetry
takes us out of ourselves. Its primary faculty, the imagination, not only
makes the absent present but makes the hidden open, as Shelley
reminds us, by allowing us to enter the lives of others, to see the world
for a moment through eyes very different from our own. Such a prac-
tice is crucial for democracies, for societies that try to base social order
on plurality, on the inclusion of the disparate rather than on a unifor-
mity of belief and behavior. And such a practice is crucial in promoting
understanding between nations, especially between nations whose gov-
ernments thrive on demonizing the enemy, among which America's
government, from time to time at least, has to be included.

My poem "More Poetry" was inspired in part by meeting two Iranians who teach American literature in a provincial high school in a small town in Iran. I was moved by their faith in the power of poetry to break down divisions between peoples. I would like to believe that a similar faith inspires some teachers here.

Contributors

Kim Addonizio was born in Washington, D.C. Among her honors are fellowships from the National Endowment for the Arts, a Guggenheim fellowship, two Pushcart Prizes, and a Commonwealth Club Poetry Medal. Her books of poetry include *Lucifer at the Starlite* (W. W. Norton, 2009); *Tell Me* (BOA Editions, 2000), which was a finalist for the National Book Award; *Jimmy & Rita* (1997, reissued 2011); and others. Addonizio is also the author of *Ordinary Genius: A Guide for the Poet Within* (W. W. Norton, 2009) and, with Dorianne Laux, coauthor of *The Poet's Companion: A Guide to the Pleasures of Writing Poetry* (1997). She has published two novels with Simon & Schuster and a collection of stories with FC2. Addonizio was a founding editor of the journal *Five Fingers Review*.

Ralph Angel was born in Seattle, Washington. He is the author of *Exceptions and Melancholies: Poems 1986–2006* (2007 PEN USA Poetry Award), *Twice Removed* (2001), *Neither World* (1995 James Laughlin Award of The Academy of American Poets), and *Anxious Latitudes* (1986) as well as a translation of the Federico García Lorca collection, *Poema del cante jondo/Poem of the Deep Song*. Recent awards include a gift from the Elgin Cox Trust, a Pushcart Prize, a Gertrude Stein Award, the Willis Barnstone Poetry Translation Prize, a Fulbright Foundation fellowship, and the Bess Hokin Award of the Modern Poetry Association. He is Edith R. White Distinguished Professor at the University of Redlands and a member of the faculty at Vermont College of the Arts. He lives in Los Angeles, California.

Mary Jo Bang was born in Waynesville, Missouri. She is the recipient of numerous awards, including a "Discovery"/The Nation award, a Pushcart Prize, a fellowship from the Guggenheim Foundation, and a Hodder Award from Princeton University. Her books *Louise In Love* and *Elegy* both received the Poetry Society of America's Alice Fay di Castagnola Award for a manuscript in progress. Bang is the author of six books of poems, including *The Bride of E* (2009), *The Eye Like a Strange Balloon* (2004), *The Downstream Extremity of the Isle of Swans*

(2001), and *Louise In Love* (2001). Her translation of Dante's *Inferno* was published in 2012. She lives in St. Louis, Missouri, where she is professor of English at Washington University.

Coleman Barks was born in Chattanooga, Tennessee. Since 1977 he has collaborated with various scholars of the Persian language (most notably, John Moyne) to bring over into American free verse the poetry of the thirteenth-century mystic Jelaluddin Rumi. This work has resulted in twenty-one volumes, including the bestselling *Essential Rumi* in 1995, two appearances on Bill Moyers's PBS specials, and inclusion in the prestigious *Norton Anthology of World Masterpieces*. In 2004 he received the Juliet Hollister Award for his work in the interfaith area. In March 2005 the U.S. Department of State sent him to Afghanistan as the first visiting speaker there in twenty-five years. In May 2006 he was awarded an honorary doctorate by the University of Tehran. In 2009 he was inducted into the Georgia Writers Hall of Fame. Barks has published seven volumes of his own poetry, including *WINTER SKY: Poems 1968–2008*. He is now professor emeritus at the University of Georgia in Athens.

Tony Barnstone was born in Middletown, Connecticut. Among his awards are the Pushcart Prize in Poetry, a fellowship from the California Arts Council, the Poets Prize, and a fellowship from the National Endowment from the Arts. He is the author of twelve books. His editions of poetry include *Tongue of War: From Pearl Harbor to Nagasaki*, winner of the John Ciardi Prize in Poetry (BKMK Press, 2009); *The Golem of Los Angeles*, winner of the Benjamin Saltman Award in Poetry (2008); *Sad Jazz: Sonnets* (2005); and *Impure: Poems by Tony Barnstone* (1999). He is a distinguished translator of Chinese poetry and literary prose, including *The Anchor Book of Chinese Poetry* (Anchor), *The Art of Writing: Teachings of the Chinese Masters* (Shambhala), *Laughing Lost in the Mountains: Poems of Wang Wei* (University Press of New England), and *Chinese Erotic Poems* (Everyman). His multimedia work includes *Tokyo Burning*, a CD of original music based on his book of WWII poems. He is the Albert Upton Professor of English at Whittier College.

Willis Barnstone was born in Lewiston, Maine. He has received the NEA, NEH, Emily Dickinson Award of the PSA, four Book of the Month selections, and four Pulitzer for Poetry nominations. His center is poetry, but his books range from memoir, literary criticism, gnosticism, and biblical translation to the anthologies. His publications include, *Poetics of Translation* (Yale, 1995), *Life Watch* (2003), *Border of a Dream: Selected Poems of Antonio Machado* (2004), *Restored New Testament* (2009), *Stickball on 88th Street* (2011), *The Poems of Jesus Christ* (2012). He is a Distinguished Professor Emeritus of Comparative Literature at Indiana University. He lives in Northern California.

Marvin Bell was born in New York City and grew up in Center Moriches, on the south shore of eastern Long Island. Bell's debut collection of poems, *Things We Dreamt We Died For*, was published in 1966 by the Stone Wall Press, following two years of service in the U.S. Army. His following collections include *A Probable Volume of Dreams* (1969); a Lamont Poetry Selection of the Academy of American Poets; and *Stars Which See, Stars Which Do Not See* (1977), which was a finalist for the National Book Award. His nineteenth book was the wartime collection *Mars Being Red* (2007), which was a finalist for the *Los Angeles Times* Book Award. His twentieth was a collaboration titled *7 Poets, 4 Days, 1 Book* (2009), coauthored with poets from Hungary, Malta, Russia, and Slovenia as well as the U.S. In 2011 he published *Vertigo: The Living Dead Man Poems* (Copper Canyon) and *Whiteout*, a collaboration with photographer Nathan Lyons (Lodima). He served forty years on the faculty of the Iowa Writers' Workshop and two terms as Iowa's first poet laureate, and he now teaches for the brief-residency MFA program based in Oregon at Pacific University. He has long lived in both Iowa City and Port Townsend, Washington.

Charles Bernstein was born in New York City. His honors and awards include the Roy Harvey Pearce/Archive for New Poetry Prize and fellowships from the New York Foundation for the Arts, the Guggenheim Foundation, and the National Endowment for the Arts. Among his more than twenty books of poetry are *Girly Man* (University of Chicago Press, 2006), *With Strings* (2001), *Republics of Reality: 1975–*

1995 (2000), *Dark City* (1994), and *Rough Trades* (1991). He is also the author of three books of essays: *My Way: Speeches and Poems* (1999), *A Poetics* (1992), and *Content's Dream: Essays 1975–1984* (1986). He has edited many anthologies of poetry and poetics. Among his translations from the French are *Red, Green, and Black* (1990, by Olivier Cadiot) and *The Maternal Drape* (1984, by Claude Royed-Journoud). Bernstein serves as the executive editor, and cofounder, of the Electronic Poetry Center at SUNY–Buffalo. Currently, he is professor of English at the University of Pennsylvania.

Christopher Buckley was raised in Santa Barbara, Califronia. His awards include an NEA grant, a Fulbright Award in Creative Writing to Yugoslavia, four Pushcart Prizes, and two Pennsylvania Council on the Arts Grants. From 1992–93 he was a Pew Fellowship in the Arts Disciplinary Winner in Poetry. His books of poetry include: *Blue Autumn* (1990), *Dark Matter* (1993), *A Short History of Light, Camino Cielo (*1997), and *Fall From Grace* (1998). His most recent book is *Rolling in the Bones* (University of Tampa Press, 2010). Buckley is professor and chair of the Creative Writing Department at the University of California Riverside.

Robert Bly was born in Madison, Minnesota. His honors include Guggenheim, Rockefeller, and National Endowment for the Arts fellowships. He is the author of more than thirty books of poetry, including *Talking into the Ear of a Donkey* (W. W. Norton, 2011), *Reaching Out to the World: New and Selected Prose Poems* (2009); *My Sentence Was a Thousand Years of Joy* (2006); *The Night Abraham Called to the Stars* (2001); *Snowbanks North of the House* (1999); and *Loving a Woman in Two Worlds* (1987). Bly introduced many unknown European and South American poets to an American audience. He is also the editor of numerous collections including *Mirabai: Ecstatic Poems* (2004), *The Soul Is Here for Its Own Joy: Sacred Poems from Many Cultures* (1995), and *Leaping Poetry* (1975).

Marilyn Chin was born in Hong Kong and raised in Portland, Oregon. Chin has won numerous awards for her poetry, including ones from the Radcliffe Institute at Harvard, the Rockefeller Foundation, and the National Endowment for the Arts. She has received a Stegner Fellowship, the PEN/Josephine Miles Award, four Pushcart Prizes, the Paterson Prize, and a Fulbright Fellowship to Taiwan. Her books of poetry include: *Rhapsody in Plain Yellow*, *The Phoenix Gone, The Terrace Empty*, and *Dwarf Bamboo* (1987). She is also the author of a novel, *Revenge of the Mooncake Vixen* (2009). In addition to writing poetry, she has translated poems by the modern Chinese poet Ai Qing and cotranslated poems by the Japanese poet Gozo Yoshimasu. She codirects the MFA program at San Diego State University.

Billy Collins was born in New York City. His honors and awards include fellowships from the New York Foundation for the Arts, the National Endowment for the Arts, and the Guggenheim Foundation. In 1992, he was chosen by the New York Public Library to serve as "Literary Lion." He is the author of several books of poetry, including *Ballistics* (2008); *She Was Just Seventeen* (2006); *The Trouble with Poetry* (2005); *Nine Horses* (2002); *Sailing Alone Around the Room: New and Selected Poems* (2001); *Picnic, Lightning* (1998); *The Art of Drowning* (1995), which was a finalist for the Lenore Marshall Poetry Prize; *Questions About Angels* (1991), which was selected by Edward Hirsch for the National Poetry Series; *The Apple That Astonished Paris* (1988); *Video Poems* (1980); and *Pokerface* (1977). He served as poet laureate of the United States from 2004 to 2006.

Carl Dennis was born in St. Louis, Missouri. A recipient of Pulitzer Prize and the Ruth Lilly Prize, he has been awarded numerous honors and awards for his work, including fellowships from the Guggenheim Foundation and the National Endowment for the Arts. He has taught at the State University of New York–Buffalo since 1966, where he is both a professor of English and writer in residence. Dennis has published numerous books of poetry, including *House of My Own* (1974); *The Outskirts of Troy* (1988); *Meetings with Time* (1992); *Practical Gods* (2001), for which he won the Pulitzer Prize; and *Callings* (2010). Dennis has also published a book of criticism, *Poetry as Persuasion* (2001).

Stuart Dischell was born in Atlantic City, New Jersey. He is the author of *Good Hope Road, Evenings & Avenues, Dig Safe,* and *Backwards Days*—published by Penguin. His poetry has won awards from the National Poetry Series, the National Endowment for the Arts, the North Carolina Arts Council, and the John Simon Guggenheim Foundation. He teaches in the Master of Fine Arts Program in Creative Writing at the University of North Carolina at Greensboro.

Sharon Doubiago was born and raised in southern California. Two weeks after completing *Hard Country,* inspired by the American gender themes she embarked on a bus journey with her fifteen-year-old daughter to Macchu Picchu. *South America Mi Hija* was nominated twice for National Book Award and was named the Best Book of the Year by the *LA Weekly.* Her other books include the poetry collections *Psyche Drives The Coast* (for which she won the Oregon Book Award for Poetry), *Body and Soul* (which includes her third Pushcart Prize winner), and *Love on the Streets: Selected and New Poems* (2008)—and her memoir *My Father's Love* (2009 and 2011). She's been a visiting writer at many colleges and an online mentor in creative writing for the University of Minnesota's Split Rock Program.

Rita Dove was born in Akron, Ohio. She served as poet laureate of the United States and consultant to the Library of Congress from 1993 to 1995 and as poet laureate of the Commonwealth of Virginia from 2004 to 2006. She has received numerous literary and academic honors, among them the 1987 Pulitzer Prize in Poetry, the 2003 Emily Couric Leadership Award, the 2001 Duke Ellington Lifetime Achievement Award, the 1997 Sara Lee Frontrunner Award, the 1997 Barnes & Noble Writers for Writers Award, the 1996 Heinz Award in the Arts and Humanities, and the 1996 National Humanities Medal. In 2006 she received the Common Wealth Award of Distinguished Service, in 2007 she became a Chubb Fellow at Yale University, in 2008 she was honored with the Library of Virginia's Lifetime Achievement Award, and in 2009 she received the Fulbright Lifetime Achievement Medal and the Premio Capri (the international prize of the Italian "island of poetry"). Most recently, President Barack Obama presented her with the 2011 National Medal of Arts. She has published the poetry collections *The Yellow House on the Corner* (1980), *Museum* (1983), *Thomas and Beulah* (1986), *Grace Notes* (1989), *Selected Poems* (1993), *Mother Love* (1995), *On the Bus with Rosa Parks* (1999), *American Smooth* (2004), *Sonata Mulattica* (2009), a book of short stories, *Fifth Sunday* (1985), the novel *Through the Ivory Gate* (1992), essays under the title *The Poet's World* (1995), the play *The Darker Face of the Earth* (1994), and most recently edited the *Penguin Anthology of Twentieth-Century American Poetry* (2011). She holds the chair of Commonwealth Professor of English at the University of Virginia.

Norman Dubie was born in Barre, Vermont. He is the recipient of the PEN USA prize for best poetry collection in 2001. Dubie's most recent collection of poems, *The Volcano*, was published by Copper Canyon Press. His other books include *The Mercy Seat: Collected and New Poems 1967–2001 (2004)*, *Ordinary Mornings of a Coliseum (2004)*, *The Mercy Seat: Collected & New Poems 1967–2001 (2001)*, *Selected and New Poems (1986)*, and *The Clouds of Magellan (1992)*. He teaches at Arizona State University.

Annie Finch was born in New Rochelle, New York. She is a poet, memoirist, translator, and librettist and is the author and editor of numerous volumes. She is the author of five collections of poetry including *Spells: New and Selected Poems* (Wesleyan University Press, 2013), *Among Goddesses: An Epic Libretto in Seven Dreams* (2010), and *Eve* (1997). She has also published several influential books of poetics, including *The Body of Poetry: Essays on Women, Form, and the Poetic Self* and *A Poet's Craft: A Comprehensive Guide to Making and Sharing Your Poem* (2012). Her music, art, theater, and opera collaborations have shown at such venues as American Opera Projects, Carnegie Hall, Chicago Art Institute, Poets House, and the Metropolitan Museum of Art. Finch's book of poetry *Calendars* was shortlisted for the Foreword Poetry Book of the Year Award, and in 2009 she was awarded the Robert Fitzgerald Award. Her epic *Among the Goddesses* was the first winner of the Sarasvati Award from the Association for the Study of Women and Mythology. She holds degrees from Yale University, the University of Houston, and Stanford University and currently directs the Stonecoast MFA program in creative writing at the University of Southern Maine.

Carolyn Forché was born in Detroit, Michigan. Her honors include fellowships from the Guggenheim Foundation, the Lannan Foundation, and the National Endowment for the Arts. In 1992 she received the Charity Randall Citation from the International Poetry Forum. She is now director of the Lannan Center for Poetry and Poetics and holds the Lannan Chair in Poetry at Georgetown University in Washington, D.C. Forché's books of poetry include: *Blue Hour* (HarperCollins, 2004); *The Angel of History* (1994), which received the *Los Angeles Times* Book Award; *The Country Between Us* (1982), which received the Poetry Society of America's Alice Fay di Castagnola Award and was the Lamont Poetry Selection of The Academy of American Poets; and *Gathering the Tribes* (1976), which was selected for the Yale Series of Younger Poets by Stanley Kunitz. She is also the editor of *Against Forgetting: Twentieth-Century Poetry of Witness* (1993). Among her translations are Mahmoud Darwish's *Unfortunately, It Was Paradise: Selected Poems* with Munir Akash (2003), Claribel Alegria's *Flowers from the Volcano* (1983), and Robert Desnos's *Selected Poetry* (with William Kulik, 1991). Forché teaches in the MFA program at George Mason University in Fairfax, Virginia.

Carol Frost was born in Lowell, Massachusetts. Her awards and honors include two fellowships from the National Endowment for the Arts, four Pushcart Prizes, and a Teacher/Scholar Award and grants from Hartwick College. Frost has taught most recently at SUNY Potsdam, New England College, Bucknell University, and Rollins College. She is the author of numerous books of poetry including: *Honeycomb: Poems* (Triquarterly Books, 2010), *The Queen's Desertion* (2006), *I Will Say Beauty* (2003), and *Love and Scorn: New and Selected Poems* (2000). Tupelo Press will publish her new book *Trilogy* in 2014. She is the Theodore Bruce and Barbara Lawrence Alfond Professor of English at Rollins College, in Winter Park, Florida.

Dana Gioia was born in Los Angeles. He is the author of *Pity the Beautiful* (Graywolf Press, 2012); *Interrogations at Noon* (2011), winner of the American Book Award; *The Gods of Winter* (1991); and *Daily Horoscope* (1986). His critical collection, Can *Poetry Matter?: Essays on Poetry and American Culture* was a finalist for the National Book Critics

Award in Criticism. Since then, Gioia has published two other collections of criticism, *Barrier of a Common Language: An American Looks at Contemporary British Poetry* (2003) and *Disappearing Ink: Poetry at the End of Print Culture* (2004). He has coedited two anthologies of Italian poetry and four of the nation's best-selling college literature textbooks. From 2003 to 2009 he served as the chairman of the National Endowment for the Arts. He is currently the Judge Widney Professor of Poetry and Public Culture at the University of Southern California.

Nikki Giovanni born in Knoxville, Tennessee, and grew up in Lincoln Heights, an all-black suburb of Cincinnati, Ohio. She is the recipient of some twenty-five honorary degrees, she has been named Woman of the Year by *Mademoiselle* magazine, *The Ladies Home Journal*, and *Ebony* magazine. She was tapped for the Ohio Women's Hall of Fame and named an Outstanding Woman of Tennessee. Giovanni has also received Governor's Awards from both Tennessee and Virginia. She was the first recipient of the Rosa L. Parks Woman of Courage Award, and she has also been awarded the Langston Hughes Medal for poetry. Her books include her autobiography, *Gemini*, a finalist for the National Book Award, *Love Poems, Blues: For All the Changes, Quilting the Black-Eyed Pea, Acolytes, Bicycles: Love Poems,* and *Hip Hop Speaks to Children: A Celebration of Poetry with a Beat.* She is a University Distinguished Professor at Virginia Tech in Blacksburg, Virginia.

Jori Graham was born in New York City. Her many honors include a John D. and Catherine T. MacArthur Fellowship and the Morton Dauwen Zabel Award from the American Academy and Institute of Arts and Letters. Graham is the author of twelve collections of poetry, including *PLACE* (Ecco, 2012), *Sea Change* (2008), *Never* (2002), *Swarm* (2000), and *The Dream of the Unified Field: Selected Poems 1974–1994,* which won the 1996 Pulitzer Prize for Poetry. She has also edited two anthologies, *Earth Took of Earth: 100 Great Poems of the English Language* (1996) and *The Best American Poetry 1990.* She is currently the Boylston Professor of Rhetoric and Oratory at Harvard University.

Marilyn Hacker was born in New York City. She is the author of twelve books of poems, including *Names* (Norton, 2009), *Essays on Departure* (Carcanet Press, 2006), and *Desesperanto* (Norton, 2003) and an essay collection *Unauthorized Voices* (University of Michigan Press, 2010). Her eleven volumes of translations from the French include Marie Etienne's *King of a Hundred Horsemen* (Farrar Strauss and Giroux, 2008), which received the 2009 American PEN Award for Poetry in Translation; Hédi Kaddour's *Treason* (Yale University Press, 2010); and Vénus Khoury-Ghata's *Nettles* (The Graywolf Press, 2008). For her own work, she is a past recipient of the Academy of American Poets' Lenore Marshall Award for *Winter Numbers*, the National Book Award for *Presentation Piece*, an Award in Literature from the American Academy of Arts and Letters in 2004, the American PEN Voelcker Award for poetry in 2010, and the Argana Prize from Morocco's Bayt as-Sh'ir in 2011. She is a chancellor of the Academy of American Poets. She lives in Paris.

Kimiko Hahn born in Mt. Kisco, New York. She is the author of eight books of poems including *Earshot* (1992), which was awarded the Theodore Roethke Memorial Poetry Prize and an Association of Asian America Studies Literature Award; *The Unbearable Heart* (1995), which received an American Book Award; *Volatile* (1999); *Mosquito and Ant* (1999); and most recently *The Narrow Road to the Interior* and *Toxic Flora* (W. W. Norton, 2011). Her latest honor is a Guggenheim Fellowship. She teaches in the MFA Program in Creative Writing and Literary Translation at Queens College, City University of New York.

Sam Hamill was born in Utah. He has been the recipient of fellowships from the National Endowment for the Arts, the Guggenheim Foundation, the Woodrow Wilson Foundation, the U.S.-Japan Friendship Commission, two Washington Governor's Arts Awards, the Stanley Lindberg Lifetime Achievement Award for Editing, and the Washington Poets Association Lifetime Achievement Award for poetry. Hamill is the author of fourteen volumes of poetry including *Almost Paradise: Selected Poems & Translations* (Shambhala, 2005), *Dumb Luck* (2002), *Gratitude* (1998), and *Destination Zero: Poems 1970–1995* (1995) and three collections of essays and two dozen volumes translated from ancient Greek, Latin, Estonian, Japanese, and Chinese. He cofounded Copper Canyon Press with Tree Swenson and was editor there from 1972 through 2004. In January 2003, he founded Poets Against War, editing an anthology with the same name (Nation Books, 2003).

Michael S. Harper was born in Brooklyn, New York. He was the first poet laureate of Rhode Island (1988–1993) and has received many other honors, including a fellowship from the Guggenheim Foundation and a National Endowment for the Arts Creative Writing Award. He has published more than ten books of poetry, most recently *Selected Poems* (ARC Publications, 2002); *Songlines in Michaeltree: New and Collected Poems* (2000); *Honorable Amendments* (1995); and *Healing Song for the Inner Ear* (1985). His other collections include: *Images of Kin* (1977), which won the Melville-Cane Award from the Poetry Society of America and was nominated for the National Book Award; *Nightmare Begins Responsibility* (1975); *History is Your Heartbeat* (1971), which won the Black Academy of Arts & Letters Award for poetry; and *Dear John, Dear Coltrane* (1970), which was nominated for the National Book Award. He is professor of English at Brown University, where he has taught since 1970. He lives in Barrington, Rhode Island.

Juan Felipe Herrera, was born in Fowler, California. A recipient of the National Book Critics Circle Award in poetry, Herrera has published in various genres. He is the author of many collections of poetry, including *Senegal Taxi: Mud Drawings* (University of Arizona Press, 2013); *Half of the World in Light: New and Selected Poems* (2008); a recipient of the PEN/Beyond Margins Award; *187 Reasons Mexicanos Can't Cross The Border: Undocuments 1971–2007* (2007); and *Crashboomlove* (1999), a novel in verse, which received the Americas Award. Herrera currently holds the Tomás Rivera Endowed Chair in the Creative Writing Department at the University of California–Riverside and is the poet laureate of California.

William Heyen was born in Brooklyn, New York, and raised in Suffolk County. A former Senior Fulbright Lecturer in American Literature in Germany, he has won NEA, Guggenheim, American Academy, and

Institute of Arts & Letters, and other fellowships and awards. He is the editor of *American Poets in 1976, The Generation of 2000: Contemporary American Poets*, and *September 11, 2001: American Writers Respond*. His books include *Pterodactyl Rose: Poems of Ecolog, The Host: Selected Poems, Erika: Poems of the Holocaus*, and *Ribbons: The Gulf War* from Time Being Books; *Pig Notes & Dumb Music: Prose on Poetry* and *Crazy Horse in Stillness*, winner of 1997's Small Press Book Award for Poetry, from BOA; *Shoah Train: Poems*, a finalist for the 2004 National Book Award, *The Confessions of Doc Williams* and *A Poetics of Hiroshima*, a Chautauqua Literary & Scientific Circle selection for 2010. He is professor of English and poet in residence emeritus at SUNY Brockport, his undergraduate alma mater.

Joy Harjo was born in Tulsa, Oklahoma. She is the author of seven books of poetry, including *How We Became Human, New and Selected Poems*, and *She Had Some Horses*, and most recently a memoir, *Crazy Brave* (W. W. Norton, 2012.) Her writing awards include the New Mexico Governor's Award for Excellence in the Arts, the Lifetime Achievement Award from the Native Writers Circle of the Americas, and the William Carlos Williams Award from the Poetry Society of America. Harjo performs nationally and internationally, solo and with her band, the Arrow Dynamics, and tours her one-woman show *Wings of Night Sky, Wings of Morning Light*. She has five CD s of music and poetry including her most recent award-winning album *Red Dreams, A Trail Beyond Tears*. She has received a Rasmuson United States Artist Fellowship and is a founding board member of the Native Arts and Cultures Foundation. Harjo writes a column Comings and Goings for her tribal newspaper, the Muscogee Nation News, and lives in the Muscogee Creek Nation of Oklahoma.

Maxine Hong Kingston was born in Stockton, California. Her first book, *The Woman Warrior*, won a National Book Critics Circle Award in 1976. Her follow-up *China Men* won the American Book Award. Her other honors include the National Humanities Medal in 1997 and the John Dos Passos Prize for Literature. Hong Kingston's other books include two novels: *Tripmaster Monkey, His Fake Book* (1989) and *Hawaii One Summer* (1998). Most recently she returned to the autobiographical with *The Fifth Book of Peace* (2003). In 2006 she edited a collection of nonfiction pieces from people touched by war in *Veterans of War, Veterans of Peace,* which were culled from some of Hong Kingston's writing workshops. She is also the author of a collection of poems, *I Love a Broad Margin to My Life* (Knopf, 2011).

Garrett Hongo was born in Volcano, Hawaii. His honors include fellowships from the Guggenheim Foundation, the National Endowment for the Arts, and the Rockefeller Foundation. His collections of poetry include *Coral Road, Yellow Light,* and *The River of Heaven,* which was the Lamont Poetry Selection of the Academy of American Poets and a finalist for the Pulitzer Prize. He is also the author of *Volcano: A Memoir of Hawai'i* (1995), and he has edited *Songs My Mother Taught Me: Stories, Plays and Memoir by Wakako Yamauchi* (1994) and *The Open Boat: Poems from Asian America* (1993). He is currently professor of creative writing at the University of Oregon at Eugene, where he directed the Program in Creative Writing from 1989 to 1993.

Andrew Hudgins was born in Killeen, Texas. His awards and honors include the Witter Bynner Award for Poetry, the Hanes Poetry Prize, and fellowships from the Bread Loaf Writers' Conference, the Ingram Merrill Foundation, and the National Endowment for the Arts. Hudgins has taught at Baylor University and University of Cincinnati. His volumes of poetry include *Ecstatic in the Poison* (Overlook Press, 2003); *Babylon in a Jar* (1998); *The Glass Hammer: A Southern Childhood* (1994); *The Never-Ending: New Poems* (1991), a finalist for the National Book Awards; *After the Lost War: A Narrative* (1988), which received the Poetry Prize; and *Saints and Strangers* (1985), which was a finalist for the Pulitzer Prize. He is also the author of a book of essays, *The Glass Anvil* (1997). He currently teaches at Ohio State University.

Richard Katrovas was born in Norfolk, Virginia. He is the founding director of the Prague Summer Program and is the author of seven books of poetry including *Green Dragons* (winner of the Wesleyan University Press New Poets Series, 1984); *Snug Harbor* (1986);

The Public Mirror (1990); *The Book of Complaints* (1993); a book of short stories, *Prague USA* (1996); a memoir, *The Years of Smashing Brick* (Carnegie Mellon University Press, 2007); *The Republic of Burma Shave* (2001); a novel, *The Mystic Pig* (2008); and *Prague Winter* (2004). Katrovas as guest editor of a special double issue of *The New Orleans Review*, edited, and participated in much of the translation of, the first representative anthology of contemporary Czech poetry, *Ten Years After the Velvet Revolution*. Katrovas taught for twenty years at the University of New Orleans and is now a professor of English at Western Michigan University.

Galway Kinnell was born in Providence, Rhode Island. He was the director of the adult education program at the University of Chicago's Downtown Center, a teacher and journalist in Iran, and a field worker for the Congress of Racial Equality in Louisiana and subsequently taught poetry at colleges in this country and abroad. A former MacArthur Fellow and State Poet of Vermont, he has been a chancellor of the Academy of American Poets. In 1982, his *Selected Poems* won both the Pulitzer Prize and the National Book Award. In 2002, he was awarded the Frost Medal by the Poetry Society of America, and in 2010 he was awarded the Wallace Stevens Award by the Academy of American Poets. Kinnell is the author of eleven books of poetry, including *Imperfect Thirst* (1994), *The Book of Nightmares(1997)*, *When One Has Lived a Long Time Alone* (1990), and most recently *A New Selected Poems* and *Strong is Your Hold* (Houghton Mifflin, 2006). He also published a novel, *Black Light*; a selection of interviews, *Walking Down the Stairs*; and a book for children as well as translations of works by Yves Bonnefoy, Yvan Goll, Francois Villon, and Rainer Maria Rilke. He taught for many years at New York University, where he was Erich Maria Remarque Professor of Creative Writing. He lives in northern Vermont.

Eloise Klein Healy was born in El Paso, Texas, and grew up in rural Iowa. Healy has published numerous collections of poetry, including *The Islands Project: Poems for Sappho* (2007); *Passing* (2002), a finalist for both the Lambda Literary Award in Poetry and Publishing Triangle's Audre Lorde Lesbian Poetry Prize; *Artemis in Echo Park*

(1991), which was also nominated for the Lambda Book Award; and *New & Selected Poems & Recordings* (Red Hen Press, 2012). As an editor, Healy is also active in the world of small-press publishing. She cofounded ECO-ARTS, a venture combining ecotourism and the arts and in 2006 established Arktoi Books, an imprint with Red Hen Press specializing in the work of lesbian writers. Healy has taught at California State University Northridge, where she directed the Women's Studies Program, and at the Feminist Studio Workshop in the Woman's Building in Los Angeles. She was the founding chair of the MFA program at Antioch University Los Angeles, where she won the inaugural Horace Mann Award. Healy lives in California.

Yusef Komunyakaa was born in Bogalusa, Louisiana. His thirteen books of poetry include *Taboo* (2006); *Dien Cai Dau* (1988), based on his experiences in Vietnam; *Neon Vernacular* (1993), for which he received the Pulitzer Prize; *Warhorses* (2009); and most recently *The Chameleon Couch* (Farrar, Straus, and Giroux, 2012). He has been the recipient of numerous awards including the Wallace Stevens Award, the William Faulkner Prize (Universite Rennes, France), the Ruth Lilly Poetry Prize, the Kingsley Tufts Award for Poetry, and the Poetry Society of America's Shelley Memorial Award. In addition to poetry, Komunyakaa is the author of several plays, performance literature and libretti, including *Saturnalia, Weather Wars, Wakonda's Dream, Testimony*, and *Gilgamesh*, which have been performed in venues including the 92nd Street Y in New York City, Opera Omaha in Nebraska, and the Sydney Opera House in Australia. He is a professor and Distinguished Senior Poet at New York University.

Maxine Kumin was born in Philadelphia, Pennsylvania. She has received the Pulitzer Prize, the Aiken Taylor Award for Modern Poetry, an American Academy of Arts and Letters award, the Sarah Joseph Hale Award, the Levinson Prize, a National Endowment for the Arts grant, the Eunice Tietjens Memorial Prize from *Poetry*, and fellowships from the Academy of American Poets, and the National Council on the Arts. She has published numerous books of poetry, including *Where I Live: New & Selected Poems 1990–2010* (W. W. Norton, 2010); *Still to Mow* (2009); *Jack* (2003); *The Long Marriage* (2003); *Bringing Together*

(2003); *Connecting the Dots* (1996); and *Up Country: Poems of New England* (1972), for which she received the Pulitzer Prize. She is also the author of a memoir, *Inside the Halo and Beyond:The Anatomy of a Recovery* (W. W. Norton, 2000); four novels; a collection of short stories; more than twenty children's books; and five books of essays, most recently *The Roots of Things: Essays* (2009) and *Always Beginning: Essays on a Life in Poetry* (2000). She has served as consultant in poetry to the Library of Congress and poet laureate of New Hampshire and is a former chancellor of the Academy of American Poets. She lives in New Hampshire.

Dorianne Laux was born in Augusta, Maine. Her most recent collections are *The Book of Men* (W. W. Norton, 2011), and *Facts about the Moon* (2005). A finalist for the National Book Critics Circle Award and winner of the Oregon Book Award, The Paterson Prize and The Roanoke-Chowan Award for Poetry, Laux is also author of *Awake, What We Carry,* and *Smoke* from BOA Editions. She teaches poetry in the MFA Program at North Carolina State University and is founding faculty at Pacific University's lowresidency MFA Program.

Philip Levine was born in Detroit, Michigan. In 2012 he succeeded W. S. Merwin as the poet laureate of the United States. He honors and publications include *News of the World* (Alfred A. Knopf, 2010); *Breath* (2004); *The Mercy* (1999); *The Simple Truth* (1994), which won the Pulitzer Prize; *What Work Is* (1991), which won the National Book Award; *New Selected Poems* (1991); *Ashes: Poems New and Old* (Atheneum, 1979), which received the National Book Critics Circle Award and the first American Book Award for Poetry; *7 Years From Somewhere* (1979), which won the National Book Critics Circle Award; *The Names of the Lost* (1975), which won the 1977 Lenore Marshall Poetry Prize from the Academy of American Poets; and *They Feed They Lion* (1973). Levine is also the recipient of the Ruth Lilly Poetry Prize, the Harriet Monroe Memorial Prize from Poetry, the Frank O'Hara Prize, and two Guggenheim Foundation fellowships. For two years he served as chair of the literature panel of the National Endowment for the Arts. He taught for many years at California State University, Fresno, and has served as Distinguished Poet in Residence for the Creative Writing Program at New York University.

Thomas Lux was born in Northampton, Massachusetts. He has been a finalist for the *Los Angeles Times* Book Award in Poetry and has received three National Endowment for the Arts grants and a Guggenheim Fellowship. His books of poetry include *God Particles* (Houghton Mifflin, 2008); *The Cradle Place* (2004); *The Street of Clocks* (2001); *New and Selected Poems, 1975–1995* (1997), which was a finalist for the 1998 Lenore Marshall Poetry Prize; *The Blind Swimmer: Selected Early Poems, 1970–1975* (1996); *Split Horizon* (1994), for which he received the Kingsley Tufts Poetry Award; *The Drowned River* (1990); *Half Promised Land* (1986); *The Glassblower's Breath* (1976); *Memory's Handgrenade* (1972). Lux has been the poet in residence at Emerson College (1972–1973) and a member of the writing faculty at Sarah Lawrence College and the Warren Wilson MFA Program for Writers. He has also taught at the Universities of Iowa, Michigan, and California at Irvine, among others. He is currently Bourne Professor of Poetry at the Georgia Institute of Technology in Atlanta, Georgia.

David Mason was born in Bellingham, Washington. Mason's collections of poetry include *The Buried House* (1991), winner of the Nicholas Roerich Poetry Prize; *The Country I Remember* (1996), winner of the Alice Fay Di Castagnola Award; *Arrivals* (2004); and the verse novel *Ludlow* (2007), awarded the Colorado Book Award for Poetry and named best book of poetry in 2007 by the *Contemporary Poetry Review* and the National Cowboy and Western Heritage Museum. Mason's prose includes a memoir about Greece, *News from the Village: Aegean Friends* (2010), and two collections of essays. He has coedited the anthologies of poetry *Rebel Angels: 25 Poets of the New Formalism* (1996), *Twentieth Century American Poetry* (2004), and *Western Wind: An Introduction to Poetry* (2005) as well as the essay collection *Twentieth Century American Poetics: Poets on the Art of Poetry* (2003). Also an opera librettist, Mason teaches at Colorado College. He was appointed the Colorado poet laureate in 2010.

Christopher Merrill was born in Northampton, Massachusetts, and raised in New Jersey. He has published four collections of poetry, including *Brilliant Water* and *Watch Fire*, for which he received the Peter I. B. Lavan Younger Poets Award from the Academy of American

Poets; many translations and edited volumes; and five books of nonfic-
tion, among them, *Only the Nails Remain: Scenes from the Balkan Wars*
and *The Tree of the Doves: Ceremony, Expedition, War*. His work has
been translated into twenty-five languages, his journalism appears
widely, and his awards include a knighthood in arts and letters from the
French government. He directs the International Writing Program at
the University of Iowa.

Stanley Moss was born in Woodhaven, New York. He is the critically
acclaimed author of *The Skull of Adam* (1979), *The Intelligence of
Clouds* (1989), *Asleep in the Garden* (1997), *A History of Color* (2003),
Rejoicing: New and Selected Poems (2006), and *God Breaketh Not All
Men's Hearts Alike: New and Collected Poems* (2011). In 1977 Moss
founded Sheep Meadow Press, a nonprofit press devoted to poetry,
with a particular focus on international poets in translation. He lives in
Clinton Corners, New York.

Carol Muske-Dukes was born in St. Paul, Minnesota. Her awards
include a Guggenheim, NEA, Library of Congress award, Castagnola
award (Poetry Society of America), Ingram/Merrill, Dylan Thomas—
and she was been a National Book Award finalist as well as an *LA Times*
Book Prize finalist and six time Pushcart Prize winner. She is the author
of eight books of poems, four novels, two collections of essays and is
coeditor of two anthologies. Her most recent book of poems is *Twin
Cities* (Penguin, 2011). Also published in 2011 was *Crossing State Lines:
An American Renga* (coedited with Bob Holman), a conversation poem
among fifty-four American poets (FSG). She is professor of English and
creative writing at the University of Southern California where she
founded the Ph.D. program in Creative Writing and Literature. She
recently completed her term as poet laureate of California.

Naomi Shihab Nye was born in St. Louis, Missouri, to a Palestinian
father and an American mother. She has written or edited thirty-three
books, including *You and Yours* (BOA Editions, 2005), as well as *19
Varieties of Gazelle: Poems of the Middle East* (2002), a collection of new
and selected poems about the Middle East; *Fuel* (1998); *Red Suitcase*
(1994); and *Hugging the Jukebox* (1982). She lives in San Antonio, Texas.

Alicia Suskin Ostriker was born in Brooklyn, New York. She has received awards and fellowships from the NEA, the Guggenheim and Rockefeller foundations, the Poetry Society of America, and the San Francisco State Poetry Center, among others. Her collections of poetry include *The Book of Life: Selected Jewish Poems, 1979–2011* (University of Pittsburgh Press, 2012); *The Book of Seventy* (2009); *The Volcano Sequence* (2002); *The Little Space: Poems Selected and New, 1968–1998* (1998) which was a finalist for the 1999 Lenore Marshall Poetry Prize; *The Crack in Everything* (1996), which was a National Book Award finalist and won both the Paterson Poetry Award and the San Francisco State Poetry Center Award; and *The Imaginary Lover* (1986), winner of the William Carlos Williams Award of the Poetry Society of America. Her numerous books of critical writing include *Dancing at the Devil's Party: Essays on Poetry, Politics and the Erotic* (2000), *The Nakedness of the Fathers: Biblical Visions and Revisions* (1994) and *Stealing the Language: The Emergence of Women's Poetry in America* (1986). Ostriker has taught in the low-residency Poetry MFA program of Drew University and New England College. She lives in Princeton, New Jersey, is professor emerita of English at Rutgers University.

Molly Peacock was born in Buffalo, New York. She is the author of six books of poems, including *The Second Blush*, as well as works of nonfiction, including *The Paper Garden: An Artist Begins Her Life's Work at 72.* She is a mentor at Spalding University's brief-residency MFA Program, edits *The Best Canadian Poetry in English,* appears in *The Oxford Book of American Poetry,* and has toured with a one-woman show *The Shimmering Verge.* Her poetry and essays are widely anthologized, including in *The Best of the Best American Poetry* and *The Best American Essays.* As former president of the Poetry Society of America, she was one of the creators of New York's City Poetry in Motion program, coediting *Poetry In Motion: One Hundred Poems From the Subways and Buses.* A dual citizen of Canada and the U.S., she lives in Toronto.

Barbara Ras was born in New Bedford, Massachusetts, and has received fellowships from the John Simon Guggenheim Memorial Foundation, the Bread Loaf Writers' Conference, the Artist Foundation of San Antonio, and the Rockefeller Foundation. Her first collection of poems, *Bite Every Sorrow* (LSU Press, 1998), was chosen by C. K. Williams to receive the 1997 Walt Whitman Award. *Bite Every Sorrow* was subsequently awarded the Kate Tufts Discovery Award. In 1999, Ras was named Georgia Poet of the Year. Her other books of poetry include *One Hidden Stuff* (2006) and *The Last Skin* (2010), which won the best poetry book of the year award from the Texas Institute of Letters. She is also the editor of a collection of short fiction in translation, *Costa Rica: A Traveler's Literary Companion* (Whereabouts Press, 1994). Ras has taught at writing programs across the country and has been on the faculty of the MFA Program for Writers at Warren Wilson College. Ras currently lives in San Antonio, where she directs Trinity University Press.

James Ragan was born in Duquesne, Pennsylvania. He is the recipient of numerous poetry honors, including three Fulbright Professorships (Yugoslavia, China, and the Czech Republic), the Emerson Poetry Prize, eight Pushcart Prize nominations, a Poetry Society of America Gertrude Claytor Award, and the Swan Foundation Humanitarian Award. Ragan's books include *In the Talking Hours* (2004), *Womb-Weary* (1990), *The Hunger Wall* (1996), *Lusions* (1997), and *Too Long a Solitude* (2009). He is also the coeditor of *Yevgeny Yevtushenko: Collected Poems, 1952–1990.* He served for twenty-five years as director of USC's Professional Writing Program and for sisteen years as Distinguished Professor at Charles University in Prague.

Tom Sleigh was born in Mount Pleasant, Texas. His books include *After One* (1983), winner of the Houghton Mifflin New Poetry Prize; *Waking* (1990); *The Chain* (1996); *The Dreamhouse* (1999); *Far Side of the Earth* (2003), an Honor Book Award from the Massachusetts Society for the Book; *Bula Matari/Smasher of Rocks*; a translation of Euripides' *Herakles*; a book of essays, *Interview With a Ghost*; and *Space Walk*, winner of the $100,000 2008 Kingsley Tufts Award; and most recently *Army Cats* (Graywolf Press, 2011). He has also received the Shelley Prize from the Poetry Society of America, the John Updike Award and an Academy Award from the American Academy of Arts and Letters, an Individual Writer's Award from the Lila Wallace Fund, and grants from the Guggenheim Foundation and the National

Endowment for the Arts. He teaches in the MFA Program at Hunter College and lives in Brooklyn.

Gerald Stern was born in Pittsburgh, Pennsylvania. His honors include the *Paris Review*'s Bernard F. Conners Award, the Bess Hokin Award from Poetry, the Ruth Lilly Prize, four National Endowment for the Arts grants, and fellowships from the Academy of American Poets, the Guggenheim Foundation, and the Pennsylvania Council on the Arts. Stern is the author of 15 books of poetry including *In Beauty Bright* (W. W. Norton, 2012), and *This Time: New and Selected Poems*, which won the 1998 National Book Award. He was elected a Chancellor of the Academy of American Poets in 2006. For many years a teacher at the University of Iowa Writers' Workshop, Stern now lives in Lambertville, New Jersey.

David St. John was born in Fresno, California, in 1949. His many books of poetry include: *The Auroras* (HarperCollins, 2012); *The Face: A Novella in Verse* (2004); *Prism* (2002); *In the Pines: Lost Poems* (1999); *Study for the World's Body: New and Selected Poems* (1994), which was nominated for the National Book Award; *Terraces of Rain: An Italian Sketchbook* (1991); *No Heaven* (1985); *The Shore* (1980); and *Hush* (1976). He is also the author of a volume of essays and interviews, *Where the Angels Come Toward Us* (White Pine Press, 1995) and has edited numerous collections including *The Pushcart Book of Poetry* (2006) and *American Hybrid: A Norton Anthology of New Poetry* (2009) which he coedited with Cole Swenson. St. John currently lives in Los Angeles, where he teaches in the English Department at the University of Southern California.

Natasha Trethewey was born in Gulfport, Mississippi. She is the author of four collections of poetry, *Domestic Work* (2000), *Bellocq's Ophelia* (2002), *Native Guard* (2006)—for which she was awarded the Pulitzer Prize—and, most recently, *Thrall* (2012). Her book of nonfiction, *Beyond Katrina: A Meditation on the Mississippi Gulf Coast*, appeared in 2010. She is the recipient of fellowships from the National Endowment for the Arts, the Guggenheim Foundation, the Rockefeller Foundation, and the Bunting Fellowship Program of the Radcliffe

Institute for Advanced Study at Harvard. She is Charles Howard Candler Professor of English and Creative Writing at Emory University.

Quincy Troupe was born in St Louis, Missouri. He is professor emeritus at the University of California, San Diego, and taught in Columbia University's Graduate Writing program. He also served as poet laureate of the state of California. His ten books of poetry include *Errancities* (Coffee House Press, 2012); *The Architecture of Language* (2006); *Transcircularities: New and Selected Poems* (2002); *Choruses* (1999); *Avalanches* (1996); and *Snake-Back Solos: Selected Poems 1969–1977* (1979), which received an American Book Award. He is also the author of *Miles: The Autobiography* (1989), which received an American Book Award; *James Baldwin: The Legacy* (1989); and the memoir, *Miles and Me: A Memoir of Miles Davis* (2000). Troupe edited the anthology *Giant Talk: An Anthology of Third World Writing* (1975) and is the editor of *Black Reneaissance Noire*. In 1991, Troupe received the Peabody Award for coproducing and writing the radio show *The Miles Davis Radio Project,* and in 2010 he was the recipient of the American Book Award's Lifetime Achievement Award for sustained literary excellence. He lives in Harlem, New York.

Brian Turner was born in Visalia, California. He is a soldier-poet who is the author of two poetry collections, *Phantom Noise* (2010) and *Here, Bullet* (2005) which won the 2005 Beatrice Hawley Award, the New York Times "Editor's Choice" selection, the 2006 Pen Center USA Best in the West award, and the 2007 Poets Prize, among others. Turner served seven years in the US Army, to include one year as an infantry team leader in Iraq with the 3rd Stryker Brigade Combat Team, 2nd Infantry Division. In 2009, Turner was selected as one of fifty United States Artists Fellows.

Jean Valentine was born in Chicago, Illinois. She has been awarded grants and fellowships from the Rockefeller Foundation, the National Endowment for the Arts, the New York State Council on the Arts, the Guggenheim Foundation, and the Bunting Institute. In 2000, she received the Shelley Memorial Prize from the Poetry Society of America. She is the recipient of the 2009 Wallace Stevens Award from the Academy of American Poets. In 1964, Valentine's first book *Dream*

Barker was chosen for the Yale Series of Younger Poets. Her recent collections include *Break the Glass* (Copper Canyon Press, 2010); *Lucy* (2009); *Little Boat* (2007); *Door in the Mountain: New and Collected Poems* (2004), which won the National Book Award; *The Cradle of the Real Life* (2000); *Growing Darkness, Growing Light* (1997); *The River at Wolf* (1992); and *Home Deep Blue: New and Selected Poems* (1989). She is also the editor of *The Lighthouse Keeper: Essays on the Poetry of Eleanor Ross Taylor* (Seneca Review, 2001). Valentine taught at New York University until 2004, and in recent years has also taught workshops and seminars at the 92nd Street Y, the University of Pittsburgh, Sarah Lawrence College, the Fine Arts Work Center in Provincetown, and Columbia University. She lives in New York City.

Charles Harper Webb was born in Philadelphia, and grew up in Houston. Among Webb's awards are the Morse Poetry Prize, the Kate Tufts Discovery Award, the Felix Pollock Prize, the Benjamin Saltman Prize, a Whiting Writer's Award, and a Guggenheim fellowship. His numerous books of poetry include *Reading the Water* (1997), *Tulip Farms & Leper Colonies* (2001), *Shadow Ball: New & Selected Poems* (2009), *Amplified Dog* (2006), and *Stand Up Poetry: An Expanded Anthology* (2002), which he edited. A former rock singer/guitarist, he is a licensed psychotherapist and directs the MFA Program at California State University, Long Beach.

David Wagoner was born in Massillon, Ohio. He has published nineteen books of poems, most recently *After the Point of No Return* (Copper Canyon Press, 2112). He has also published ten novels, one of which, *The Escape Artist*, was made into a movie by Francis Ford Coppola. He won the Lilly Prize in 1991, six yearly prizes from *Poetry*, two yearly prizes from *Prairie Schooner*, and the Arthur Rense Prize for Poetry from the American Academy of Arts and Letters in 2011. In 2007, his play *First Class* was given forty-three performances at A Contemporary Theatre in Seattle. He was a chancellor of the Academy of American Poets for twenty-three years. He edited *Poetry Northwest* from 1966 to 2002, and he is professor emeritus of English at the University of Washington. He teaches at the low-residency MFA program of the Whidbey Island Writers Workshop.

Sholeh Wolpé was born in Tehran, Iran, and has lived in Trinidad, England, and the United States. Her publications include three collections of poetry—*Keeping Time With Blue Hyacinths* (University of Arkansas Press, 2013), *Rooftops of Tehran* (2008), and *The Scar Saloon* (2004)—and two books of translations—*Sin: Selected Poems of Forugh Farrokhzad* (2007), which was awarded the 2010 Lois Roth Translation Prize, and Walt Whitman's *Song of Myself* which she cotranslated into Persian with Mohsen Emadi. Wolpé is the editor of two anthologies, *The Forbidden: Poems from Iran and Its exiles* (Michigan State University Press, 2012) and *Breaking the Jaws of Silence: Sixty American Poets Speak to the World* (University of Arkansas Press, 2013). She was a regional editor of *Tablet & Pen: Literary Landscapes from the Modern Middle East* (Norton, 2010).

Robert Wrigley was born in East St. Louis, Illinois, and grew up in Collinsville, a coal mining town. Wrigley's awards and honors include fellowships from the National Endowment for the Arts, the Idaho State Commission on the Arts, and the Guggenheim Foundation as well as the J. Howard and Barbara M. J. Wood Prize, the Frederick Bock Prize from *Poetry* magazine, the Wagner Award from the Poetry Society of America, the Theodore Roethke Award from *Poetry Northwest,* and six Pushcart Prizes. From 1987 until 1988 he served as the state of Idaho's writer in residence. His collections of poetry include *Beautiful Country* (Penguin, 2010); *Earthly Meditations: New and Selected Poems* (2006); *Lives of the Animals* (2003); *Reign of Snakes* (1999), winner of the Kingsley Tufts Award; *In the Bank of Beautiful Sins* (1995), winner of the San Francisco Poetry Center Book Award and Lenore Marshall Award finalist; *What My Father Believed* (1991); *Moon in a Mason Jar* (1986); and *The Sinking of Clay City* (1979). He has taught at Lewis & Clark College, the University of Oregon, twice at the University of Montana (where he returned to hold the Richard Hugo Chair in Poetry), and at Warren Wilson College. He teaches in the MFA program in creative writing at the University of Idaho.